Rural Monsters, Myths and Legends

By Liz Carey

Copyright © 2022, 2023 by Liz Carey

All rights reserved.

Originally published pieces in The Daily Yonder
www.dailyyonder.com

Book design, Cover design – Liz Carey

First Paperback Edition

ISBN   9798355548544

CONTENTS

THE BOGGY CREEK MONSTER 9

BIGFOOT 19

MOTHMAN 31

THE MONSTER OF LAKE PEPIN 41

CATTLE MUTILATIONS 45

DIANA OF THE DUNES 53

KENTUCKY'S ALIEN INVASION 63

THE SNALLYGASTER 69

THE BIG MUDDY MONSTER 77

THE FLATWOODS MONSTER 83

IOWA'S VAN METER VISITOR 93

INDRID COLD 99

THE GEORGIA GUIDESTONES 109

STRANGE FEMALE LEGENDS 119

MODERN MYTHS 131

BLUE-EYED INDIANS 147

THE DARK WATCHERS 153

The Boggy Creek Monster

The Legend and Legacy of Boggy Creek

Back in the summer of 1975, I watched a movie that would change my life. It wasn't an Oscar winner. It wasn't an inspirational tale about a horse or a dog or an orphan going on to do overcome incredible odds. It wasn't even an action-adventure film set in a galaxy far, far away.

It was a low-budget docu-drama and it scared the heebeejeebees out of me – "The Legend of Boggy Creek."

Back then, I was a tow-headed 10-year-old with pony tails called "Mary Beth." A tomboy at heart, I was all tennis, and shorts, and swimming, and riding horses bareback through the woods behind my friend's house way out in the sticks of Woodford County in Central Kentucky. I wasn't scared of anything, even if I didn't know anything about anything yet.

That summer, as I remember it, my cousins, Gene and

Roger, were visiting our house and we all went to the drive-in to see a movie - "The Legend of Boggy Creek." My aunt says it was probably my Dad piling everyone into the station wagon so we could save money and take our own popcorn and drinks. How they managed to talk my always protective mom into letting me see it, I'll never know.

What I do know is that the movie not only scared me silly, it ignited a lifelong obsession with rural legends that lives on to this day.

The Legend of Boggy Creek centers around the real story of a monster terrorizing townspeople in Fouke, Arkansas. Mixing staged interviews with re-enactments of their encounters with a Bigfoot-like swamp creature, the film recounts stories that have circulated about the Fouke Monster for decades

The Fouke Monster, also known as the Boggy Creek Monster and the Swamp Stalker, was first reported in the news in 1971. Residents in the Fouke area of Arkansas said the monster was at least 7 feet tall, if not 10 feet tall, weighing anywhere between 300 and 800 pounds. It ran with a swift, galloping gate, swinging its arms like an orangutang and smelling like "a combination of skunk and wet dog," witnesses said. Footprints in the area said to belong to the creature measured some 17 inches long and featured only three toes.

The creature first made the news when Bobby and Elizabeth Ford told the *Texarkana Gazette* they'd spotted something in the fields outside of their house. According to Elizabeth Ford, the creature reached through a screen window while she was sleeping on a couch. Bobby and his brother Don said they chased the creature away, shooting at it from the porch. Later, the group found three-toed footprints close to the house, as well as damage to the house's porch, window and siding.

A few days later, the creature was sighted again. This time D.C. Woods, Jr., Wilma Woods and Mrs. R. H. Sedgass said they saw it crossing U.S. Highway 71. Over the next few months, more sightings followed, with both locals and tourists spotting the creature and finding more footprints. Scott Keith, the owner of a local filling station, reported finding Fouke Monster tracks in his soybean field.

As news of the Fords' encounter spread, radio station KAAY posted a $1,090 bounty on the monster, drawing hunters and their dogs to Fouke. The dogs weren't able to track the creature, but the proliferation of guns in the area led Miller County Sheriff Leslie Greer to put a temporary "no guns" policy in place for safety purposes. The sheriff fined three people $59 each for "filing a fraudulent monster report."

After a while, interest in the monster faded out and sightings dwindled off. One local man, however, never stopped wondering about it. Local resident Charles B. Pierce started asking questions about the Fouke Monster. His investigation would be the beginning of "The Legend of Boggy Creek."

Born in 1938, Pierce grew up in Hampton, Arkansas, just a few miles away from Fouke in the southwestern part of the state near Texarkana. As a child, he was a friend and neighbor to Harry Thomason. As children,

Thomason and Pierce would make movies together in their backyards using an old 8-mm camera.

Pierce went on to be art director for KTAL-TV in Shreveport, Louisiana, and later serve as a weatherman and host a children's cartoon show for the same channel. Thomason went on to be a film and television producer and director. He's most known for his work with his wife, Linda Bloodworth Thomason, on the television series "Designing Women."

In 1969, Pierce moved to Texarkana and bought a 16-mm camera to start an advertising agency. One of his first gigs was with Ledwell & Son Enterprises, a company that built 18wheel trailers and farm equipment. The commercials he shot for them went on to solidify his reputation locally for his creative abilities.

After interviewing several of Fouke residents about their encounters with the monster, Pierce decided their authenticity and down-to-earth qualities would make a great movie. While he didn't necessary believe in the tales of the Fouke Monster, he said he was fascinated by tales of encounters with it. Working with Earl E. Smith, an acquaintance from advertising, he adapted the interviews into a screenplay.

Then Pierce turned to his client, L. W. Ledwell, owner of Ledwell & Sons. With his script and movie idea in hand, Pierce asked if he'd finance his movie. Although he was skeptical of the idea, he agreed to loan Pierce $100,00 to make his movie.

Pierce's total move budget was only $160,000, the equivalent of about $1.13 million in today's dollars. To put that in context, "The Godfather," which was also released in 1972 cost $6 million to make the equivalent of about $42 million today. The Godfather would go on to gross $135 million in 1972. Pierce's low-budget production would go on to make $20 million – a 12,400% return on his meager investment.

It was an extremely local production. Shooting the film in Fouke, Texarkana and Shreveport, Pierce used the interviews with Fouke residents and mixed them with dramatizations of their encounters with the monster. He hired high school students to be crew members and found his actors at the local gas station, where he would approach those who looked like someone that he wanted in his movie. He wrote and sang the theme song himself. Once shooting for the movie was done, he packed it in his trunk and headed to Hollywood for help with post-production services.

Unfortunately, while he could get back-end services done for a small upfront fee and a percentage of the box office receipts, the rest of Hollywood wasn't as interested in the film. No one wanted to distribute it. So, like he did with everything else, he decided to figure out how to show it by himself. Renting a local movie theater in Texarkana, later called the Perot Theater, Pierce premiered the film on August 23, 1972.

Here's the thing - when it opened, there were lines stretched around the block to see it. In its first three weeks it made more than $55,000. Pierce never expected it to become a financial success. Within months though, he was in a distribution deal with Howco, an independent distribution company, for $1.29 million and a 50 percent interest in the film. Later, Pierce and Howco signed a deal with American International Pictures for foreign and television distribution. The film would go on a few years later to become a hit at drive-in movies across the country and gain a cult status.

Which is where my nightmare fuel comes in.

In the movie, residents talk about how the creature has killed several large animals over the years, with one farmer saying the beast had carried off two of his 100-pound hogs. One scene implies that the creature scares a kitten to death. Later, the monster terrorizes a family with a daughter named... wait for it... Mary Beth.

It was a pivotal scene for me. The on-screen Mary Beth is scared by noises she hears outside that she's sure are made by the monster. She retreats inside the house and hides. As she's looking out the window, the monster breaks through and reaches out for her.

Yeah. Scared the hell out of me. In my 10-year-old mind, that was me! It was coming after ME!

That night, I remember Roger and Gene making fun of me as we drove home, but also telling me that everything was going to be okay. I had a trundle bed in my room at the time – like a bunk bed, but the bottom bunk rolled out from under the bed to sit on its own. Roger and Gene, there to keep me safe, slept on the beds and I slept under the upper bunk – surrounded by my cousins protecting me.

I still remember dreaming that night that the monster was outside of my window, sitting on the garage roof, waiting to break through the window and come in and get me.

As dusk broke into dawn though, my feelings changed. That morning, all I could talk about was the movie. Was it real? There's no way another animal could scare a kitten to death, was there? Did they really see what they thought they saw? Is it still out there? And if it is real, why hasn't anyone captured it yet?

And most importantly, how could something like that happen in a small town?

At the time, we lived in Versailles, Kentucky, a rural town about a half an hour from Lexington. The landscape is dotted with horse farms and for the most part, all 21,000 of us knew each other. The idea that something like that could happen in a small town thrilled me. Nothing ever happened in Versailles. The most exciting thing to do was drive from the Dairy Queen (where all the cool kids worked) to the Circle K near the old elementary school and back again. Why couldn't something exciting like a monster happen in MY hometown?

It was the beginning of my fascination with cryptids, monsters, myths and rural legends.

In high school, my friends and I would hunt for the ghost who lived in our local library. We tracked down an abandoned house that somehow still had lights on and dared each other to climb the front steps and knock on the door. And we'd go to the edge of the county to find

"Scaly Man," a boy who, legend said, was born with no epidermis.

According to the legend, after driving down Scaly Man's long driveway out in the middle of nowhere (naturally), you were supposed to park your car in front of his house, turn out the car lights, honk three times and wait for him to appear... Of course we did it all to the letter. And we thought for sure he came out... My friend tried to start her car, but the engine wouldn't turn over. Fear turned to panic, and we were all sure we were going to die. There was a lot of screaming until the car finally turned on. Once we'd peeled out of Scaly Man's driveway, the screams turned to breathless babbling about what we'd just seen and giggling over our adventures.

Since then I've gone to Point Pleasant to visit Mothman, and found out as much as I can about all sorts of legends - from South Carolina's Lizard Man to the Minnesota Hodag. The television series "Monsters, Myths and Legends," as well as "Fact or Faked" and "The UnXplained" with William Shatner are some of my go-to shows. The old 90s series "Unsolved Mysteries" is on almost every morning as background noise while I write.

But more than just a fascination with the stories, I was fascinated with whether or not they were real. The older I got, the more I looked at witness statements with a skeptical eye. In 2012, I visited the Georgia Guidestones about an hour away from my house in Anderson, S.C. and used my investigative reporter skills to dig into how the project was funded, who bought and sold the land and who the Guidestones mysterious benefactor was.

Fast-forward to 2021 and the midst of the pandemic. At the time, I was one of the rural health reporters for the Daily Yonder, a national news outlet covering rural issues only out of the Center for Rural Strategies in Whitesburg, Kentucky. I had spent a year writing about Covid-19, the lack of medical resources, overwhelmed hospitals, mental health struggles, drug overdoses and death. I needed a break from the bad news. So, I asked my editor if I could write about how one of the Bigfoot shows was hunting for him in rural Kentucky.

That story led to others – Mothman; the Flatwoods Monster; Little Green Men in Kelly, Kentucky; Diana of the Dunes in the Indiana Dunes National Park; winged creatures who terrorized small towns and even cattle mutilations in the American West. They were a hit, drawing attention from all over the globe. One of our stories – about a $50,000 reward for proof of Pepie the Lake Pepin Sea Monster – even got reprinted in Scotland.

After a year, we had a collection of stories we published as a series. And now, we've compiled them into a book and added other stories – like this one on the Legend of Boggy Creek.

Back in 1973, I had no idea of the impact that one movie would have on me. But it certainly started a lifelong fascination with the unexplained that I'm sure will continue to draw me into investigating all sorts of rural myths, legends and monsters.

Bigfoot

The Search for Bigfoot in Kentucky

Of all the things you'd expect to find in the hills of Kentucky, proof of Bigfoot's existence might not be at the top of your list.

But in 2021, a team of paranormal researchers and reality TV show investigators thought Kentucky's southeastern mountains might have the key to proving the cryptid is out there and roaming around in Appalachia.

In early 2021, the crew of the Travel Channel's TV show "Expedition Bigfoot" filmed their third season in Kentucky, and think they may have found proof of Bigfoot DNA.

The team – Bryce Johnson (expedition operations), Dr. Mireya Mayor (primatologist), Russell Acord (ex-military/survivalist) and Ronny LeBlanc (Bigfoot researcher) – uses the latest technology to search for the elusive cryptid. From drone footage to trail cams to on-the-ground investigations, the group collects data and sends it to experts to analyze.

And it's not just a team of amateurs and enthusiasts out combing the woods either. Johnson, Acord and LeBlanc have extensive histories as Bigfoot researchers, while Dr. Mayor is a world-renowned primatologist.

For nearly 20 years, Dr. Mayor has been a wildlife correspondent for several journals, including National Geographic. Her explorations have led to several scientific discoveries, most notably the co-discovery of a new species of primate, Mittermeier mouse lemur, the world's smallest.

The team first visited Harlan County, Kentucky in 2020. Representatives of the show contacted Harlan County historian and author Darla Saylor Jackson, and Harlan paranormal researcher Tony Felosi. The two were able to put the team in the right places at the right time, even getting them in touch with a former pastor and employee of the Kentucky State Police, Tony Turner, who gave the team an audio account of his encounter with a suspected Bigfoot creature.

During the second season of Expedition Bigfoot, six episodes took place in Harlan County. The researchers used high-tech equipment to track the creature into the hills, getting responses to their Bigfoot calls, finding structures built by the cryptids and discovering large footprints in a hidden cave.

By analyzing reports of Bigfoot sightings, the group was able to identify what appeared to be migratory routes for Bigfoot creatures running through the area.

In the third season, in 2021, the team returned to the Kentucky mountains.

Using an advanced algorithm, the team calculated the location of a 75,000-acre area in southeast Kentucky with the greatest mathematical odds of encountering a Bigfoot during a specific 21-day window.

Starting there, they were able to find the cryptid's migratory route, as well as a possible structure made from trees similar to what others claim Bigfoot creatures make. Those structures were key to identifying whether the Bigfoot creatures did live in the area.

According to Sasquatch Investigations of the Rockies, tree structures are thought to be an indication of Bigfoot creatures (also known as Sasquatches) marking off their territory from other Bigfoot creatures.

To determine whether Bigfoot had stayed there, the team collected soil samples from under the structures and sent them to the UCLA California Environmental DNA program for analysis. Environmental DNA (eDNA) is genetic material naturally left behind by animals in the environment. Researchers analyze eDNA samples to generate a snapshot of whatever animals or creatures are living in the area.

What they found wasn't what you'd expect to find in the hills of eastern Kentucky.

According to Miroslava Munguia Ramos, the eDNA program project manager, analysis of the sample indicated another primate other than humans had been in the structure.

"What we're looking at are the unique organisms that we were able to identify. Our software does what's known as metabar coding. So, it'll match up all the DNA sequences that we were able to detect and try to cross reference them with the thousands of genomes that have been published...," she said. "What I found very interesting was that, yes, we have detected human DNA in these areas, but we're still seeing different primate DNA. There wasn't just one human primate, but several different primates, some sort of primate relative that exists in the data."

Ramos said the DNA seemed to come from a species of chimpanzee not normally seen in the rural hillsides of Kentucky.

"It's a real head scratcher," she said. "It's important to note that the higher the detection, the more confidence we can say that whatever organism, whatever taxonomy we're looking at was apparent in the area."

In fact, what they found was more than 3,000 reads, or 3,000 DNA fragments, for the Pan or Chimpanzee genus. For Dr. Mayor, the discovery is significant because it's based on science, not on lore or legend.

"Finding what appears to be a very large structure, seemingly created with intention and requiring great strength as well as foresight, is interesting. It is not unheard of for primates to stack sticks or rocks, although for me, the jury is still out as to what that was," Dr. Mayor said. "There is no guesswork in science. It is great that eDNA was collected from that site. That may give us the answers we are looking for."

Dr. Mayor said the DNA find was surprising.

"Since living things shed DNA, eDNA gives you a snapshot of anything that has been in the area. In this case, one of the samples taken from under the tree structure surprisingly yielded chimp DNA, and unsurprisingly, human DNA as well as hawks, deer and other animals you'd expect to find there," she said.

Chimps are apes, she said, and it was unlikely an ape was living in the Appalachian Highlands.

"The DNA findings do not suggest a new species, but rather a match to known species of chimpanzee," she said. "Because there are no known non-human primates in North America, this is an extremely surprising find, and one that warrants further investigation."

But the investigative team is a long way off from declaring that they've found proof Bigfoot exists, she said. They are, however, a little bit closer.

"The process of describing and confirming a new species is difficult. DNA is absolutely essential in the scientific community to prove that something is a new or recognized species," she said. "You have eyewitness accounts from tens of thousands of people who say they have encountered Bigfoot, some coming forward with blurry videos and photographs. But that is just not going to cut it. What we need is indisputable genetic evidence to really put this mystery to rest. And there's no doubt in my mind that we are headed in the right direction."

The team's discovery isn't something that surprises Thomas Marcum.

Marcum, the founder of The Crypto Crew, a cryptozoology and paranormal research group based in Kentucky, said he's seen Bigfoot in southeastern Kentucky for years. Marcum used his experiences seeing, hunting and researching Bigfoot to write the book "Understanding Bigfoot: Helpful Information and Answers to Common Questions."

"Yes, Bigfoot is real," he said. "I've seen it on several occasions. They are not dumb animals but very intelligent beings that have a language… Over the years, I have had many things happen, spoken with thousands of witnesses, found a lot of evidence of these forest people… At this stage in my life, I spend massive amounts of time in the mountains. When I first started getting into Bigfoot, I was on the fence about if it was real or not, but I was able to answer that question for myself."

Marcum said one of the misconceptions of Bigfoot is that it only lives in certain parts of the country, like the Pacific Northwest. He said he's had plenty of Bigfoot sightings in his home state, starting when he was a teenager.

"My first encounter happened when I was 15 years old," he said. "My father and I were coon hunting and we had something pace us on the side of the mountain. Our dogs were terrified and so were we. At the time, I didn't know or understand what was pacing us, but years later I figured it out."

In 2013, he said, he not only got a clearer view of Bigfoot — he got a picture.

"It was a cold and snowy day," he said. "We got about 2-3 inches of wet snow. We live in a very heavily wooded area with forest in front (of) and behind our house. I looked out the window and saw this very large, I'd guess around 10-foot-tall, black-haired creature walking on the side of the mountain. I was maybe 100 yards away, with a clear view. This very large black figure stepped in between two large trees, moved off to the right and up a small ravine."

Marcum wonders if large mounds he has seen in and around Bell and Harlan counties in Southeastern Kentucky could be the graves of deceased cryptids. Grave sites, he said, may be the reason why no one ever reports finding Bigfoot skeletons. Marcum said he has come across two large mounds of dirt and rocks about 30- to 40-feet apart, deep in the woods of Kentucky.

"One of the reasons why we may not find Bigfoot bones often is that they bury their dead," he wrote on the Crypto Crew blog.

Marcum said he's not saying the mounds absolutely are Bigfoot grave sites, but wonders whether they could be.

"This is in an area where I have had several Bigfoot encounters and found many tracks," Marcum said. "Now of course, I have no idea if these are really graves or just odd humps of dirt on the ground. It could be nothing more than a natural formation or something a person did a long time ago. I have not and would not dig into them. But I am confident that Bigfoot does bury their dead."

According to Marcum, it should come as no surprise to him that Bigfoot might choose the Bluegrass State to live in.

"The area is not subject to extreme cold temperatures," he said. "There is an abundance of food and water sources. There are plenty of natural caves and old coal mines for shelter. I have researched extensively in Harlan county and it is a prime area for Bigfoot. Kentucky in general has long been a hotspot for Bigfoot sightings and encounters. The state rarely gets any recognition of this fact though as many think that Bigfoot is only out in California, Oregon and Washington. This is not true at all."

Since posing his question, Marcum has gotten some heat over whether or not the mounds were Bigfoot graves.

But, he counters, he never said they were. He just posed the question.

"I have spoken with many witnesses and researchers, and the general consensus is that Bigfoot bury their dead," he said. "If a Bigfoot grave site could be found and dug up it probably wouldn't change a whole lot within the cryptid community. Most who have a genuine interest in the subject already understand there is plenty of evidence confirming the creature is more than a myth... The mounds I have run across over the years could be nothing. I have never claimed them to be Bigfoot graves. What are they? I don't know. I was only sharing what I had found and asking a question as to what they could be and if others had found anything similar."

Over the course of 2021, Bigfoot sightings have boomed across the country. Witnesses reported Bigfoot sightings in Georgia, Idaho, Illinois, Missouri, Ohio and Pennsylvania in 2021 to name just a few.

In Ohio, an Ashland County man reported seeing a Bigfoot creature in his backyard, just a few months after another Ashland County resident said they saw a Bigfoot near a 24hour gym.

The man, who asked not to be named, told the *Richland Source* he saw a large, dark figure come out of the woods behind his home and walk along the tree line of his property. According to a report he filed with the "Finding Bigfoot" television show, after a 90-minute rain in June, the man was on his riding lawn mower when he saw something along the tree line near a field of soybeans he had recently planted.

The figure walked out, crossed the bean field and then returned to the woods.

Although he normally would have had his phone with him, he didn't have it on him at that moment, he told the paper.

"It had been raining hard right before I mowed. I normally keep the phone in my pocket, but I didn't want to have it with me in case it started raining again," the man said. "It happened so quickly. There would have been no way for me to get back into the house and grab it. I knew it would be gone."

The man said he had hoped trail cams would pick up the figure, but it stayed just out of range of the camera, following a deer trail.

Later, he said, he tried to find footprints for the creature, but found none. Two depressions near a creek could have been footprints, he said, but weren't clear enough to tell for sure.

Following the sighting, he tried to re-enact the encounter using his 5' 11", 235-pound son, but it was clear from the way his son walked, the encounter wasn't with a human.

A few months earlier, a 20-year-old woman in the area said she saw something she couldn't explain after an April evening workout.

According to her report, she was leaving the Warehouse 24Hour Gym in Ashland, Ohio around midnight when she heard a twig snap. Turning to look, she saw a seven- or eight-foot-tall creature covered in gray fur running to the woods. Shaken, she called her parents and asked them to come and pick her up.

Marcum said he thinks the uptick in sightings is

due to more awareness and people getting outside during the pandemic.

"I think that social media has played a part by bringing people who have an interest in the subject together. This also brought more awareness to the topic, more people are looking, more people feel comfortable coming forward," he said. "But also we have more people out in the forest than in years gone by. We have more people hiking, birdwatching and enjoying nature."

In Kentucky, he said, the forests are recovering from years of strip mining and over-logging, leaving animals, including Bigfoot creatures, to thrive in the area.

"In my part of Kentucky, the black bear population is really doing well but I can remember back when we had no or very few bears in this area. Now you are subject to see one just about at any time," he said. "As our forests become healthier, we see animal populations increase. This is no different for Bigfoot. A healthier forest means it can support more animal species. A healthier forest has an increased carrying capacity for living creatures, which would include Bigfoot. And this increase would lead to more sightings."

While Expedition Bigfoot returned to the West coast for its third season, it's unclear if they will return to eastern Kentucky to find the elusive cryptid. What is clear is that some evidence - whether it's from DNA or sightings - suggests that Bigfoot, or something like him, is living in the hills of the Bluegrass state.

Mothman

A Tribute to West Virginia's Mothman Continues

After two years off for the Covid-19 pandemic, organizers for the Mothman Festival couldn't wait to bring the event back.

The festival takes place in mid-September where Mothman was originally seen - Point Pleasant, West Virginia.

The creature's rise from frightening flying monster to tourism draw includes everything from a bridge disaster to a Richard Geer movie.

Sightings of Mothman began in rural West Virginia in the late 1960s.

Chris Rizer, executive director for Main Street Point Pleasant and president of the Mason County Historical Society, said the first reported sighting of Mothman may have actually been in Clenendin, West Virginia, about 70 miles southeast of Point Pleasant.

According to local legend, two grave diggers were working in a graveyard when they saw a large, winged man flying overhead.

But the legend really took off on November 15, 1966, when two couples out driving near a World War II munitions plant outside of town reported something they couldn't explain.

The creature, they said, was a large man with wings flying in the night sky. The couples said that whatever it was followed them as they drove home and had glowing red eyes.

The next day, a story in the *Point Pleasant Register* titled "Couples See Man-Size Bird... Creature... Something" kicked off a string of similar sightings.

> "Steve Mallette of 3305 Jackson Avenue and Roger Scarberry of 809 30th Street described the thing as being about six or seven feet tall, having a wingspan of 10 feet and red eyes about two inches in diameter and six inches apart," the story read. "'It was like a man with wings,' Mallette said. 'It wasn't like anything you'd see on TV or in a monster movie...'"

> "The men and their wives were in Scarberry's car between 11:30 p.m. and midnight when they spotted the creature near the old power plant next to the old National Guard Armory buildings," the story continued. "The creature was seen standing on three occasions and was described as being extremely fast in flight but was a clumsey (sic) runner."

Deputy Millard Halstead said he had seen dust in the vicinity of a coal field. But "it could have been" caused by a bird, he told the paper.

According to the Register, the men swore they hadn't been drinking. Police officers investigated and found nothing.

"I'm a hard guy to scare," Scarberry told the Register. "But last night I was for getting out of there."

They said the creature had a head that was "not an outstanding characteristic," and that whatever it was followed them as they tried to drive out of town. Both men said the creature was grayish in color and scurried through a field before taking off to fly over the couples' car. they described the creature's eyes as glowing red when lit up by their lights, but whatever it was, they said, seemed scared of the light.

Despite the scare, the men said they'd return to the site to look for the creature the next night.

Over the next three days, residents reported another eight sightings of the creature. As crowds flooded the nearby McClintic Wildlife Refuge, volunteer firefighters had to keep crowds at bay.

Two volunteer firemen said they saw a "large bird with red eyes."

Mason County Sheriff George Johnson said he thought the sightings were of an unusually large heron. Dr. Robert L. Smith, associate professor of wildlife biology at West Virginia University, agreed. In follow-up stories about the incident, he told the Gettysburg Times the creature was likely a sandhill crane that had wandered out of its migration route.

A contractor some 100 miles away even reported seeing the creature. Newell Partridge of Doddridge County said he saw something about 90 minutes before the Point Pleasant sightings — something he said was responsible for the disappearance of his dog.

Partridge said he was inside his house when his television "started acting like a generator," and his German Shepherd, Bandit, started "carrying on something terrible." Partridge said he saw something in his field and shined a light on it. Once the light hit the creature, he said, his dog's hair stood up on end and it bolted into the field. Partridge said he never saw his dog again.

Over the next two weeks, more reports came in about the winged creature. In one police report, Mothman swooped down over another moving car, scaring the passengers inside. On Nov. 16, armed townspeople scoured the area around the TNT plant for Mothman. Mr. and Mrs. Raymond Wamsley, as well as Marcella Bennett and her baby daughter Teena, were visiting friends living near the TNT plant. As they were leaving, a figure appeared behind their car, slowly rising up from the ground as if it had been laying down, Mrs. Bennett said. The group ran back to the house to phone the police, but the creature, they said, followed them, stepping onto the porch and peering at them through a window.

About a week later, four more people reported seeing Mothman flying over the TNT area. The next morning, on Nov. 25, Thomas Ury reported to the Point Pleasant Sheriff's office that he was driving along Route 62, north of the TNT area, when he saw the Mothman standing in a field.

And on Nov. 26, Mrs. Ruth Foster of Charleston, West Virginia, reported the Mothman was standing in her front lawn. The next day, the creature allegedly chased a young woman near Mason during the morning, and later chased two children in St. Albans that night.

A little over a year later, the residents blamed the Mothman for the area's largest tragedy. Depending on who you talk to, the sightings are either a warning or a result of Mothman's presence.

Some believe Mothman is an Indian omen, sent to warn the city of impending doom coming as the result of an ages old curse put on Point Pleasant by Shawnee War Chief Cornstalk in the 1700s.

According to legend, Cornstalk was a Shawnee War Chief, who helped the Americans fight against the British. On Nov. 10, 1777, two militiamen were out hunting in the area when they were ambushed and killed by unknown Native Americans. In a blind fury, their leader, Captain John Hall, murdered the chiefs, including Cornstalk.

As the Native American Chief lay dying on the floor, he cursed the town and those who had betrayed him. Some think Mothman was a thunderbird sent by the Great Spirit to fulfill Cornstalk's curse.

Tales of large winged creatures aren't uncommon in

folklore, however. In Tennessee, North Carolina, and Virginia, sightings of the "belled buzzard" in the 1850s were considered omens of disaster. In the 1870s the legend of the belled buzzard moved to West Virginia, Delaware, Georgia and South Carolina, until, in 1878, the belled buzzard was seen in Brownsville, Tennessee, and was thought to be a portent of the yellow fever epidemic there.

Across the pond in England and Scotland, a creature named "Spring-heeled Jack", described as "devil-like" in appearance with claws, a cape that helped him fly and "eyes resembling red balls of fire", was said to be roaming the streets, terrorizing women and then leaping over 9-foot tall walls to get away.

The Silver Bridge Collapse

On Dec. 15, 1967, the Silver Bridge in Point Pleasant collapsed. Loaded with rush-hour traffic, a single eye bar gave out, sending cars into the icy waters of the Ohio River below. The collapse resulted in 46 deaths.

After that, sightings tapered off, but never ended completely.

"There were sightings even after the Silver Bridge disaster," said Jeffrey Wamsley, founder of the Mothman Festival and Mothman Museum in Point Pleasant. "The movie and other books always push the story ending when the bridge fell but there are documented sightings well into the 70's and 80's."

In 1975, a man named John Keel came to Point

Pleasant and learned all he could about the Mothman. Later, he published "The Mothman Prophecies," a book about his investigation into the legend. The book blended the tale of the flying cryptid with alien encounters, the Men in Black, prophecies of the bridge collapse and other paranormal activity.

For what it's worth, officials investigating the collapse found it to be anything but paranormal.

The Silver Bridge was built in 1928 to connect Point Pleasant with Gallipolis, Ohio. When it was constructed, Americans were driving Model-Ts, each of them weighing about 1,500 pounds. In 1967, the average American car weighed a little over two tons. The Silver Bridge wasn't built with a great deal of innovation or caution, either. Officials said it featured very little redundancy, meaning very few precautions were put in place to prevent collapse or failure if even one small part failed.

According to the West Virginia Department of Transportation, the original bridge design called for conventional wire cables, but that design was replaced with an eye bar chain design — a cheaper alternative. In 1966, one of the bridge's annual inspections found that it needed about $300,000 in repairs, the equivalent of about $2.5 million today.

At 5 p.m. Dec. 15, 1967, as the bridge was packed with rush hour commuters and Christmas shoppers, witnesses said they heard a loud gunshot-like noise before the bridge "folded like a deck of cards" in less than 20 seconds. The entire 1,460-foot suspended portion of the Silver Bridge collapsed into the river below it, taking with it 32 cars and claiming 46 victims.

In its 1971 report about the bridge collapse, the National Transportation Safety Board (NTSB) determined the collapse was caused by a small crack in one of the eye bars. When it was built, the NTSB said, "stress corrosion and corrosion fatigue were not known to occur in the bridge materials used under conditions of exposure normally encountered in rural areas," and that the minute crack would not have been detectable by any method except disassembling the joint.

But in the local area, the collapse was central to the Mothman legend. Known only locally for years, it wasn't something the average American knew about. In 2002 though, "The Mothman Prophecies" movie, starring Richard Gere and based on Keel's book, came out. From there, interest in the creature skyrocketed.

It was around that time town leaders decided they needed a festival to celebrate their mythical visitor.

The organizers held the first Mothman Festival in 2001. Since then, Wamsley says, the event has grown. The event begins with a kick-off event on Friday night, then runs through Sunday. The festival features vendors, cosplay, music, food, guest speakers, hay rides and tours of the area where Mothman was originally seen.

"Obviously tourism has grown and the Mothman story has drawn people from all over the world to visit the museum and statue, but it has also introduced people to Point Pleasant's rich river and

Native American history," Wamsley says. "So it's a win-win situation...not every small town has its own Mothman to attract the visitors that come here year-round."

The success of the festival gave rise to the Mothman statue in the middle of town, and later the Mothman Museum. The draw of the legend has turned the town of 4,000 into a tourist destination with museums, art galleries, antique stores, a hotel and plenty of other attractions nearby, making it a premiere tourist destination, Main Street's Chris Rizer said. Ice cream shops offer Mothman Shakes. There's even a Mothman pizza at one of the local pizza parlors.

"As my predecessor here at Main Street Charles Humphreys always said, 'Mothman is what gets them off the highway. Then we have to keep them here with everything else'," Rizer said.

It seems to be working. Rizer estimates that between 50,000 and 75,000 people come to Point Pleasant each year in search of the winged cryptid. Even when the festival was canceled due to Covid, visitors hoping to get a glimpse of the creature came to town.

"Last year (2020) was fantastic because we didn't have the festival, but everyone who was planning on coming to the festival just came whenever they could come," he said. "So I mean, you just spread those 15,000 festival-goers out over a whole year, and, you know, you might get an extra three or four people a day... Last year was a good year for Point Pleasant."

Sightings of the creature continue every two years or

so, Rizer said. In 2016, news reports from WCHA/WVAH said a man who had recently moved to the Point Pleasant-area captured photographs of what appeared to be Mothman. While the man declined an on-camera interview, his photos appeared to show a large, winged creature with human-looking legs flying through the sky. In 2020, one man even claimed to have seen Mothman at Chicago's O'Hare Airport.

Neither proven nor debunked, and whether the sightings were Mothman is still in question. That's the way people like it, Rizer said.

"It's one of those things where the main attraction is the mystery," Rizer said. "I don't think anyone really wants to know whether it's real or a hoax, just that it's, you know, sort of a possibility."

The Monster of Lake Pepin

A Reward for "Pepie" Remains Unclaimed

Once the ice begins to melt off of Lake Pepin, Larry Nielson gets ready to talk to people about something lurking beneath its blue-green waters – and he's willing to pay them if they prove it exists.

Located beside the Mississippi River, Lake Pepin is bordered by Wisconsin on one side and Minnesota on the other. In the rural town of Lake City, Minnesota on Lake Pepin's shores, tales of a monster in the lake have been floating around since the 1870s. Supposedly a large, serpent-like creature, the monster – or Pepie, as the locals call it – has been seen by everyone from the Dakota Indians to local vacationers.

Now Nielson, the owner of the 125-passenger paddlewheel boat Pearl of the Lake, and president of the Lake City Tourism Bureau, is offering a $50,000 reward for anyone who can prove Pepie exists.

Nielson said he didn't know the water serpent existed until he saw the creature a few years back.

"One night, my wife and I were out on Lake Pepin and there were no other boats out there with us," he said. "All of a sudden I saw a big wake out there against the current. It was about 100-feet long and foot and a half high. So I started doing some research and that's when I heard about Pepie."

Reports of Pepie stretch back to the Dakota Indians, who lived in the area in the 1800s, according to Chad Lewis, a cryptozoologist, researcher and author of "Pepie: The Lake Monster of the Mississippi River." When the Dakota lived in the Minnesota area, they decided to trade in their birch bark canoes for thicker dugout canoes when traveling Lake Pepin in order to protect themselves from the creatures living in the lake that punctured their thinner birch canoes.

Stories of the lake monster died off in the 1930s and 1940s. But since the beginning of the 2000s, more people have reported seeing Pepie, he said.

He's not surprised that a monster could live in the lake given its similarity to another monster-inhabited body of water – Loch Ness.

"In terms of actual physical description, it's almost identical to Loch Ness," Lewis said. "Where Loch Ness is about 23 miles long and about a mile and a half wide, Lake Pepin is 22 miles long and about two miles wide. But both are surrounded by the beautiful hills. Even though Loch Ness is much, much deeper than Lake Pepin, I always state that if you were dropped out of an airplane into one or the other, you wouldn't know which one you were in right away."

Some believe Pepie could be a sturgeon – a long, prehistoriclooking fish that can live for as long as 100 years and weigh up to 200 pounds. But others, like Nielson, believe it's a sea monster trapped inland.

Every year, Nielson said, people say they see it lurking on the water.

"We've had about seven or eight formal expeditions to try and find it," he said. "And I get a ton of calls… throughout the summer from people who say they've seen it."

It was Nielson's idea to offer the reward – in part to find out if the stories are true, and in part to boost tourism a little.

"When I first brought this up, one lady was concerned that talking about Pepie publicly would scare all the kids and that no one would want to go in the water," he said. "But then I went down to the lake and there were kids yelling into the water for Pepie to come out and play."

Collecting the reward takes a bit of doing – whoever wins it will have to produce a good photograph and a piece of the creature's fin or skin for DNA testing. But, once researchers at the University of Minnesota biology department confirm the DNA came from an unknown species in the lake, and the photo can be authenticated, Nielson said he will gladly hand over the cash.

Several people have sent Nielson pictures of the monster. One fisherman even brought in a sonar image of something 16- to 17-feet-long under his boat. But no one has ever gotten close enough to grab a bit of fin or skin.

Having seen the monster though, Nielson said he knows it's out there.

"I know there's more things in the universe that we don't know about than we do," he said. "When we find out something and we think we know it all, we find out we don't."

Lewis, the cryptozoologist who conducted his own investigation into Pepie back in 2013, said he thinks the reward has awakened something in people.

"It has been seven years since the reward for Pepie was first issued, and I never could have imagined that such a novel idea would all but resurrect an almost forgotten legend," Lewis said. "I take comfort in knowing that after hundreds of years of sightings, the Lake Pepin water serpent remains just as intriguing and puzzling as it did when the first Native people encountered it. I sincerely hope that no matter what happens, Pepie continues to keep the people on the shores of Lake Pepin on their toes."

Cattle Mutilations

Alien Experiment, Violent Crime or Natural Occurrence?

In the beginning of 2021, cattle ranchers in Central Oregon's Crook County started reporting cattle dead in the fields.

But what makes those deaths so mysterious is the condition of their bodies. The cattle corpses had no blood and no tracks from predators or other animals around them. They were missing body parts. In some places, the cattle had seemingly surgical incisions where their organs and genitalia were extracted.

And while cattle mutilations aren't new to Oregon or the West Coast, area farmers wondered what was causing the spate of dead livestock.

Theories about what is happening to the animals vary. Some say it's part of the natural decomposition process, while others blame scavengers and vandals working to hurt the ranchers by affecting their bottom line.

One expert says the cattle mutilations are the result of some out of this world experimentation.

Linda Moulton Howe, a journalist and paranormal investigator, believes the bloodless, trackless animal deaths are evidence that we are being visited by extraterrestrials. "I began investigating bloodless, trackless animal mutilations in Colorado in September 1979, when I was Director of Special Projects at the CBS station KMGH-TV in Denver, Colorado," she said.

Again and again, she said, she heard from law enforcement and other investigators that the attacks were preceded by lights in the sky.

"Law enforcement and ranchers saw strange glowing circular craft at night extend beams down into their pastures where they would find a bloodlessly mutilated animal after the sun came up," she said. "It was Sheriff Tex Graves of Logan County, Colorado, who told me in September 1979, 'The perpetrators of these animal mutilations are creatures from outer space.'"

Howe discovered as part of her investigation these kinds of cattle mutilations have gone on around the world for decades.

"I quickly learned they were not confined to Colorado," she said. "I've been in almost every state in the United States and in Canada. I talked with a producer at the BBC in London; they had found a journal that went back to 1904 in Australia where sheep were mutilated — tongues gone, genitals gone, random organs removed, but no blood."

Howe, in her book, "Alien Harvest," said incidents of cattle mutilation have been documented in every country except India.

In Oregon, Crook County Undersheriff James Savage said his department investigated the cattle mutilations.

"Well, yeah, it makes us angry," he told the Northwest News Network. "It's upsetting, because, again, it's our livelihood. It's how (farmers) make their money and how they feed their families and support themselves."

Savage said it started with a cow found in late February on private land in a remote area. Later, another six animals turned up across the county with missing body parts, he said. In most cases, the dead animal's sex organs, tongue or eyes were cleanly removed from the body with surgical-like incisions. However, law enforcement officers investigating the carcasses say the scenes appear to be bloodless.

According to the Oregonian, detectives called large animal vet Taylor Karlin in on the case. She agreed that the deaths were unnatural. Her comments were included in a search warrant request filed by detectives in the case to find cell phone activity near the incident site.

It wasn't the first-time ranchers in Oregon have reported cattle mutilations. In 2019, cases popped up all over Oregon— in Harney, Wasco, Umatilla, Wheeler and Lake counties. Those reports mirror ones reported during a rash of cattle mutilations in the late 1970s across the American West and Midwest.

And the theories behind the mutilations in 2019 were almost the same as what they thought happened in the 1970s.

Over the course of five days in October, farmers discovered five dead bulls within a mile and a half of a timbered ravine near Salem. Farmers said there was no indication that they'd been shot, attacked by predators or killed by poisonous plants. In all of them, the sex organs and tongue were missing, as was all the animals' blood.

At first, ranch managers and law enforcement suspected that the bulls were killed by a person or persons, and advised ranch hands in the area to travel armed and in pairs.

Then the calls started coming in.

Nearby rural residents proposed their theories ranging from bugs to vandals to Harney County Sheriff's Deputy Dan Jenkins. One person even suggested to Jenkins that he look for craters under the carcasses - an indication that the animals had been levitated into an alien spaceship, mutilated and then dropped back to the ground.

Jenkins led the investigation at the time and said it ran into road blocks. With no witnesses, there was no one with any concrete information about what happened. And no cases like the October one had been solved in the past, he said.

But Colby Marshall, the vice president of the Silvies Valley Ranch, said at the time he had his own theory. He believed the mutilations were being perpetrated by members of a cult.

Just like in the 1970s, speculation ran rampant that the mutilations were for nefarious purposes. Satanists, aliens and vampires were blamed 50 years ago when thousands of cattle started showing up dead in similar conditions from Minnesota to New Mexico. At the time, even U.S. senators got into the act, asking the FBI to investigate. While the agency said it lacked jurisdiction, it was able to investigate the cases that happen on tribal lands.

But then, the mutilations stopped. Former FBI agent Kenneth Rommel, lead investigator in the case, said there was no indication in the cases they looked into that anything other than common predators were to blame.

In 2019, however, farmers believed it wasn't just natural predators. Marshall, with Silvies, said if people killed the bulls, it could have been financially motivated. Breeding bulls cost thousands of dollars, and the 100-plus calves each of them sire are worth thousands more.

But, he said, the ranch employed about 75 people from the nearby community, making it unlikely that someone would target a business that impacts the local economy.

He suspected the bulls were killed for their organs.

While some animal organs are available cheap at slaughterhouses, Marshall said it looked like people had gone to great lengths to get the parts on the open range. And, he said, because the cuts appeared to be made by a knife or a scalpel, it appeared to be a perpetrator other than Mother Nature.

"To lose a completely healthy animal would be an oddity," Marshall said at the time. "To lose five young, very healthy, in great shape, perfect bulls that are all basically the same age ... that is so outside the bounds of normal activity."

In his scenario, the bulls were hit with tranquilizer darts to knock them out, and, while lookouts kept watch, the perpetrators bled the animals with large-gauge needles, then removed the organs after the heart stopped beating.

For Jenkins, the theory was similar, but for more disreputable reasons.

"Personally, I would lean more toward the occult, where people for whatever reason— whether it's a phase of the moon or whatever rituals they're going to do with their beliefs — are coming to different areas and doing that," he told NBC News.

Two years later, in 2021, sheriffs from the counties where cattle mutilations occurred worked to coordinate and share information, officials said.

If any criminal wrongdoing is found in the cattle deaths, those responsible could face possible charges ranging from criminal mischief, trespassing to aggravated animal abuse.

But some say these are all just natural deaths.

Brian Dunning, host of the long-running podcast Skeptoid, said these cases are typical of previous cattle mutilations attributed to aliens or satanic rituals. All of the mysterious elements of the cattle corpses can be explained by science, he said.

"When an animal dies in the field, predation sets in very quickly, the first responders being insects and birds," Dunning said. "The exposed soft tissue is always the first to go: eyes, lips and tongue, genitals. As the animal is dead with zero blood pressure, there is no bleeding. The exposed skin dries and shrinks tight, giving the impression of a perfect scalpel-like slice. Blowflies and other insects, whose eggs can hatch in 10 hours, fill the wounds with maggots which can expose clean, dry bone in just a few hours more."

During the height of the cattle mutilation craze in the 1970s, one sheriff decided to do his own research, Dunning said.

Dunning said the 1970s were when stories of alien autopsies and Satanic cult worship reached a fever pitch - and cattle mutilation was used as evidence for both. But some resisted the idea that it was anything other than natural causes. At least one sheriff, he said, looked at the deaths from a more scientific approach and put a fresh cow carcass out in a field to observe what happened.

"After just two days, he'd not only seen the above bird and insect effects, but the stomach split open from expanding gasses, and blowflies had completely cleaned out the internal organs," Dunning said.

The sheriff's investigation had a chilling effect on all things paranormal.

"At that point, his department stopped searching for mythical Satan worshippers," Dunning said.

Even the FBI did research into cattle mutilations during the 70s and came to the same conclusions, he said.

Dunning said that what killed the animal in the first place is a question for animal experts. Just the fact that a cow experienced some sort of mutilation after it died doesn't provide any clues on how it died, he said, and that only a necropsy (an autopsy done on an animal after its death) performed by a veterinarian could determine a cause of death.

So far, Dunning said, none of the cases where a necropsy was done has ever been found to have an extraordinary or inexplicable cause of death.

Diana of the Dunes

Indiana Dunes Oldest Ghost Story's Amazing Backstory

Walk along the shores of Indiana Dunes National Park and you may get a glimpse of one of Indiana's oldest ghosts.

For years, people have reported seeing a pale, lithe woman running along the shores the Ogden Dunes in Indiana Dunes National Park on Lake Michigan near Gary, Indiana. From the 1920s until now, visitors have reported seeing the ghostly figure of a woman running along the beach and disappearing into the water.

Locals hold that the ghost is that of Alice Gray, a woman dubbed "Diana of the Dunes" by the Chicago press, unwilling to leave her beloved home and solitary lifestyle.

Our story starts in 1916, when fishermen noticed a young woman dancing and frolicking in the water, completely nude. What once spread as a story between fishermen soon spread to reporters in nearby Chicago. Once reporters got wind of the story, the race was on to see who could find the frolicking "nymph of the dunes" first.

It didn't take long for the myth to form – reporters claimed she was the daughter of a doctor, and that she had fled society. They dubbed her "Diana of the Dunes" after the mythological Roman goddess. They described her as a hermit, foraging for food. They hounded her for interviews. They made her a local celebrity.

But the real Diana was more complicated than that. According to "Diana of the Dunes, the true story of Alice Gray," written by Janet Zenke Edwards, Diana's real name was Alice Mabel Gray. The daughter of a laborer, Alice had three brothers and two sisters, as well as a very close relationship with her mother. At the age of 16, she entered the University of Chicago where she became a member of the Phi Beta Kappa Society and graduated six years later with "honorable mentions" in astronomy, mathematics, Greek and Latin.

After college, in 1903, she went to work for the U.S. Naval Observatory as a mathematician, but left the post two years later to take graduate courses at the University of Gottingen in Germany. She returned a year later and was employed as a stenographer at the University of Chicago.

By 1915, she'd become dissatisfied with her work. She held wage-earning labor in disdain, calling it slavery, and loathed the need to constantly work to support herself in Chicago. Some reports indicate she may have had a platonic love affair with a professor at the University that went badly.

"I had a month's salary — it was $78, perhaps. Many times I have eked out a comfortable living on 11 cents a week," she told reporters at the *Chicago Tribune* in 1916. "I can eat rye bread and think I have a feast. I was tired of working under the conditions and the lighting in offices, so I came out here. Then I wished never to go back to Chicago-to the learned and the officious. Out in the dunes I wished to regain my poise once more."

She moved herself to the Indiana Dunes, taking up residence in an abandoned fishing shack she called "Driftwood." There, she lived peacefully, living off fish and berries in the park, and making trips into nearby cities to purchase supplies and borrow books from the nearby library. It appears that she edited some manuscripts for University of Chicago professors to earn money.

Once the press heard the story, they flocked to the beach after her. After all, women just didn't walk off and live alone on a beach in the early 1900s. At that time, women didn't have the right to vote yet, nor the right to own property. Reporters found an educated woman, living in a 10x20 shack with a sand floor.

On July 23, 1916, the *Chicago Examiner* ran an article about Alice. Her reason for living alone amongst the dunes? "I want to live my own life – a free life," she reportedly told them.

Within weeks, dozens of news articles told the world about "Diana of the Dunes."

"Cleaving the water like a milk white dolphin came a mermaid. She made the shallows, rose up out of the water, then like a fabled nymph, flitted off into the shadows," wrote one report in the *Lake County Times* in 1916.

The reports detailed her time on the lake and her living conditions.

> *"A colorful blue cap that she picked up on the railroad ties adorns her cupboard - a box with shelves which she says looks quite palatial when the arrangement is in order. The floor is sand, heaps and billows of it, and the curtain to the one north window is another box. She carried a window frame with two panes of glaze over the dunes not long ago and here is soon to be a real window, she said. The little shack, which she says is not quite palatial in dimensions, is called Driftwood. The name was chosen for its appropriateness, as all her furniture was driftwood, thrown out by the generous lake.*

"I had been living under the pine trees for nearly four months, when a fisherman told me of this deserted hut, which he wanted to fix up for me for $5, but I didn't have the money, so I made do with it. It is very comfortable," she told reporters. "It was much warmer than the wigwam up at 'the sweep' as I called it."

Before moving to "Driftwood," she camped out with only a tarp for protection, the small tent allowing rain in during storms that soaked her clothes and other meager possessions.

> "The night before Christmas, when there was a terrible storm and I was out under the pine trees in the snow, I repeated two prayers to keep from freezing: 'I will go unto the altar of God: into God who maketh glad my youth,'" she wrote in her journal. "I repeated while the winds howled. Then. 'Lord, I am not worthy that thou should'st enter under my roof: speak but the word and my soul shall be healed.' I repeated over and over the two prayers. the only ones I knew, and seemed to grow warm in the snow. I then thought only of the beauty of the storm till morning."

Defiantly, however, she vowed to reporters that she wouldn't stop her nude bathing. Anyone who saw her, she said, was too far away to see anything clearly.

> "I can't see why a woman, if she chooses, may not take a daily plunge without a bathing suit," she told reporters. "I glance up and down the shore and know how far away the intruders are and also know that their vision of me is blurred. I shall not discontinue my habits because a coroner or a sheriff has seen me bathing from miles afar."

The stories gained attention across the city and turned her into a celebrity. People wanted to know whether the well-educated, city-dwelling young woman could make it in such stark conditions. Visitors flocked to the area trying to see her on the dunes or view her shack from tourist boats on the lake, Edwards wrote. Alice tried to avoid them as best as she could. Her celebrity, though, did more than create an interest in her lifestyle, it created an interest in the dunes.

In fact, one report even detailed her superiority at duck hunting.

"Nimrods from this city who returned today with one lone duck as a result of duck hunt in the dunes observed with envy a score on a line at Miss Gray's windowless cabin," one newspaper account read. "During all the bright nights the wild ducks remain out on Lake Michigan. At dawn, they come flying in to seek the little marshes as their feeding grounds. Miss Gray is ready at the last ridge, and as the birds come over, she pops them right and left."

Even her forays into the city of Chicago were publicized. Editors paid her to write essays about her trips and whether or not she missed her dune home. Naturally, she said she did.

But the area was changing, and more people were moving to the dunes. Alice called it the "Gary-izing" of her beach, after the nearby town of Gary, Indiana. As developers built more houses closer and closer to the dunes, Alice began to publicly speak out about the need to preserve the dunes and the natural landscape she so loved. In an editorial, and in a talk to the Prairie Club in Chicago, Alice told of the virtues of saving the natural beauty of the dunes.

Had her story ended there, the romantic vision of a rebellious woman living life on her own terms would have wrapped up quite nicely.

Instead, Alice's life took a dark, albeit romantic, turn.

In 1920, Alice took up with a man named Paul Wilson, a local fisherman and carpenter with a history of run-ins with the police. Wilson earned money crafting handmade furniture he sold to local residents and tourists. The couple moved into another home on the dunes; this one called "Wren's Nest." Although Alice referred to Wilson as her husband, no record of their marriage has been found, historian Richard Meister said. By all accounts, Alice was happy with her "caveman" husband, as the press called him.

Things turned from good to bad for the couple around 1922, when a badly burned body was discovered on top of an oil slicked pyre near "Wren's Nest." Authorities suspected Wilson. One deputy, Eugene Frank, accusing the couple of breaking into nearby cottages and stealing fish.

Angered at the allegations, the couple confronted Frank and a fight ensued. Wilson was shot in the foot. Alice suffered a skull fracture after Frank hit her in the head with his pistol. Wilson and Frank were arrested. Alice was hospitalized.

When the two returned to "Wren's Nest" they found it ransacked. A manuscript Alice had been working on was missing. Charges were brought against Frank, but they were dropped when Alice and Wilson failed to show up in court. Wilson was also eventually cleared of any wrongdoing in the case of the dead body.

With the area becoming more developed, and their infamy growing, the couple decided to move to Texas, opting to float down the Mississippi on a 20x24 raft they built themselves with parts Wilson salvaged from a steamship. For unknown reasons, however, they returned to Ogden Dunes a few months later, Edwards writes, asking for permission from the land owner to return to their beloved "Wren's Nest."

In 1925, Alice was diagnosed with kidney disease, but opted not to receive treatment. On February 8, she died of uremia poisoning. Prior to her death, she had begged Wilson to have her cremated and have her ashes scattered amongst the tallest of the Dunes. But Wilson lacked the funds to have her cremated, and lacked the strength to carry her wishes out. Instead, her family claimed her body and buried her in a grave at Oak Lawn Cemetery in Gary. Her tombstone reads "Alice Gray Wilson."

Some say, her unsettled spirit—forever trapped in a tomb she didn't want—has settled instead on forever haunting the park, ensuring she'll never have to leave the dunes she loved.

Alice's legacy, however, lived on after her. Her advocacy for the Indiana Dunes saved the park from development. In 1966, the dunes became a unit of the National Park Service and in 2019, it became the Indiana Dunes National Park.

In honor of Alice's legacy, the park launched the Diana of the Dunes Dare, where park visitors are encouraged to walk along the three dunes Alice may have walked on.

Whether Alice went to the dunes to find a place to live, to find solitude, or to leave society is up for interpretation, said Kim Swift, director of education for Indiana Dunes National Park said.

"We just don't know," Swift said. "She was fairly successful. She obviously could take care of herself and find work. She had family including a sister in Michigan City. In terms of what drove her here, I'm not sure we know… I'm not sure we'll ever know the real answer. So many of her journals were lost when they had that altercation with Deputy Sheriff Frank."

We're not even really sure that she went skinny dipping in the lake, Swift said.

"The press at the time was really enamored with that part of it," she said. "But Alice didn't adamantly say she didn't do it, and she never said she did."

Whatever the reason, Alice left society and for nine years, lived a life like no other.

Now, if the ghost stories are true, it seems Alice is once again with her beloved dunes, "living" amidst nature again.

Kentucky's Alien Invasion

Legend of "Little Green Men" Invading Kelly, Ky. Continues

Nearly 70 years ago, a four-hour encounter between two families and a group of unidentified visitors put Kelly, Kentucky, on the paranormal map.

The incident will forever be known among paranormal enthusiasts as the first recorded incident where Earthlings came into contact with "Little Green Men."

On August 21, 1955, two families – a total of more than a dozen people – flooded into the Hopkinsville Police Department, their eyes wide with terror. Officers reported that the families were genuinely terrified.

According to police reports from the witnesses, it all started about 7 p.m.

It was a hot Sunday night on the Sutton farm, police reports indicate. The family of Lucky Sutton – which included 50year-old widow and matriarch Glennie Lankford; four of her sons, including Lucky; two of the son's wives; a brother-in-law; and the widow's three younger children ages 12, 10 and 7 – gathered in the unpainted three-room house to visit with family friend Billy Ray Taylor and his wife June. Taylor had worked with Lucky in traveling carnivals and was visiting from Pennsylvania.

Around 7 p.m., Taylor went outside to fetch some water from the backyard well. While out there, reports indicate he said he saw a silver-colored object, "real bright, with an exhaust all the colors of the rainbow." The object, he said, came silently toward the house, passed over it and then stopped in mid-air before dropping straight to the ground.

When Taylor went back into the house, the Sutton family laughed off his experience.

But, newspaper reports indicate, about an hour later, the family's dog began barking. Lucky Sutton and Taylor went to the back door to investigate and saw a strange glow in the backyard, in the middle of which was a small human-like creature, about three-and-a-half-feet tall, with an "oversized head... almost perfectly round." The creature had arms that extended almost to the ground, hands with talons on them, and oversized yellow glowing eyes. The body, they said, gave off an eerie shimmer in the light, as if made from "silver metal."

It was then that the two men grabbed their guns – a 20-gauge shotgun and a .22 rifle – and opened fire on one of the "little gray men". In response, the little man did a flip, righted himself and then fled into the darkness.

Not long after, the men reported seeing a creature in a side window of the house. They opened fire on it through the window screen, where it, once again, flipped and disappeared.

Mrs. Lankford told Isabel Davis, author of "Close Encounter at Kelly and Others of 1955," that she witnessed the creature too.

"I went out in the hallway and crouched down next to Billy, when I saw one approaching the door," Mrs. Lankford said. "It looked like a five-gallon gasoline can with a head on top and small legs. It was a shimmering bright metal like on my refrigerator."

Taylor ran out onto the porch to confront the creature, stopping under a small overhanging roof. Witnesses inside the house said a claw-like hand reached down from the roof and touched Taylor's hair. Those inside grabbed Taylor and pulled him back into the house, while Lucky shot at the overhang and then at other creatures he said he saw in trees nearby. Each time, the creatures evaded bullets and then floated to the ground before running off into the woods, the group reported.

For the next couple of hours, the group stayed inside

the house, listening to scratches on the roof, guns ready for any further "attack." Eventually, around 11 p.m., the group made a break for their cars and took off toward the Hopkinsville police station.

Once there, the eight adults and three children ran into the station. One thing was for certain, police said, they were genuinely terrified.

"These aren't the kind of people who normally run to the police for help," police chief Russell Greenwell later told the Kentucky *New Era* newspaper. "What they do is reach for their guns."

There the group told police they'd held off between 12 to 15 of the creatures for nearly four hours as the creatures repeatedly popped up in doorways and peered into windows.

Investigators descended on the farm. Hopkinsville police and state troopers came to dig into the case, but no evidence was found that indicated the farm had been visited by aliens. No tracks of "little men" were found, nor were there any marks indicating anything had landed. Investigators did find a bullet holes in the screen door and shell casings on the ground, however.

Eventually, investigators left, but apparently, the creatures didn't. The Suttons reported the men reappeared around 3:30 that morning.

Naturally, the incident was picked up by the news in the area, and then spread across the country.

Somewhere along the way, the Sutton's were misquoted and "little grey men" was turned into "little green men." It was the first time the phrase was used to describe extraterrestrials, and it has been a term for referring to extraterrestrials since.

In fact, news of the Sutton farm encounter garnered a reaction from Washington, D.C. According to Associated Press reports at the time, Senate Republicans in Congress thought the "little green men" were likely Democrats searching for candidates, and that the opposing party's members were "green with envy" at the popularity of President Dwight D. Eisenhower.

Since then the sighting has been the subject of books, TV shows and speculation.

It was a story the community finally embraced in 2010. When looking for ways to make money, the idea of a festival came up. Kelly's history came down to two themes – trains or aliens, Joann Smithey, one of the festival's organizers, told *The Washington Post*. The town, she said, chose aliens.

And for nine years, the festival drew crowds of alien aficionados, cosplayers, and tourists to the town of about 300 people. Smithey estimated that in 2017, during the solar eclipse where Kelly landed in the path of the eclipse's totality, some 21,000 people visited the town.

The Snallygaster

Cryptid Fan Hopes Museum Brings Attention to Snallygaster

F or Sarah Cooper, the hidden story of the Snallygaster is something western Maryland needs to know more about.

Cooper, the founder and owner of the American Snallygaster Museum in Libertytown, Maryland, said the cryptid's story is one that is not only an untold gem as far as rural legends go, but also a story that could bring tourism to the area.

In the 1770s, German immigrants came to western Maryland and brought with them brats, beer, dances and the Schneller Geist – or "quick spirit". Parents would whisper to one another that the Schneller Geist, a half-bird, half-reptile creature with a teeth-lined metallic beak, would sweep down from the sky to pick off livestock or people in order to suck their blood. Eventually, the name morphed into Snallygaster. To protect themselves, like they did in the old country, the immigrants painted their barns with hexes, red seven-pointed stars.

In the late 18th century, a group of lumberjacks claimed to have come upon the Snallygaster perched high on a cliff. When they investigated, they found a nest they said belonged to the Snallygaster with an egg inside of it large enough "to hatch a horse."

For nearly 140 years the legend remained a local tale, mostly used to scare children, and in some instances, to prevent slaves from running off. But by the beginning of the 20th century, the Snallygaster would rear its ugly head again.

Between January 16 and January 23, 1909, newspapers all over New Jersey published accounts from residents who claimed they'd seen the Jersey Devil. Described as a biped with wings, hooves, and a horse-like head, the Jersey Devil had been a staple in New England lore since the 1700s. Think of a kangaroo bottom with cloven-hoof feet, and a body with leathery bat-like wings, tiny arms with claw-like hands, the head of a mule with horns and a forked tail. Typically, the creature flies overhead, emitting a blood-curdling scream, legend said.

During that week, residents reported that the creature had attacked a trolley car in Haddon Heights and a social club in Camden. Other residents reported finding unidentified footprints in the snow. Sightings of the creature in South Jersey so concerned officials that schools closed and workers stayed home. Groups of men armed with rifles scoured the forests and farmlands looking for the creature.

And despite a $10,000 reward from the Philadelphia Zoo for its capture, no one ever caught it. It did, however, generate lots of press coverage and national attention. Based on the initial stories, newspapers across the region picked up the story and ran with it.

Which brings us to February 1909 and Middletown, Maryland.

According to a letter to the *Middletown Valley Register* from Thomas C. Harbaugh, a Snallygaster with a horned head and a 20-foot-long tail, had been seen and heard chasing him and screeching. For weeks after, reports of the monster peppered the local newspaper. By the end of the month, it had glowing red eyes, tentacles coming out of its mouth, razor sharp metallic talons and a roar like a locomotive. Some reported the Snallygaster had picked up a farmer, sucked the blood from his neck, and then flung his lifeless body over a cliff.

Over the course of two months, several people reported seeing the creature, and some even reported hearing fights between it and its mortal enemy, the Dwayyo: a wolf-like creature that walked on two feet.

The monster even made national news.

The stories so captured the national attention that soon people in other states were reporting they'd seen a Snallygaster. In New Jersey, one resident said they found the footprints of a Snallygaster in the snow. In West Virginia, reports came out that the Snallygaster had almost caught a woman near Scrabble, and was later found roosting in a farmer's barn where it had laid an egg the size of a barrel.

These days, there are reports that at the time, the Smithsonian offered a reward for a dead Snallygaster, and that *National Geographic* was planning an expedition to Maryland to catch a picture of the creature, and even President Teddy Roosevelt considered putting off a safari to Africa so he could go hunt through the wilds of Central Maryland to bag a Snallygaster. Where those reports came from, however, isn't clear. A spokesman for the Smithsonian says there's no record the museum ever offered a reward for the creature, or that Roosevelt ever considered putting off his trip.

But one thing is clear - it was the report of the president delaying his trip that forced George C. Rhoderick, Sr. the editor of the *Middletown Valley Register*, and his staff writer Ralph S. Wolfe, to come clean. Rhoderick and Wolfe are largely credited with starting the Snallygaster tales. While the description of the beast mimics that of monsters in German folklore, it was Rhoderick and Wolfe who brought the beast to life on the pages of the Register.

C. H. Minnebraker, the paper's publisher, admitted they'd decided to write various "eyewitness accounts" as a way to increase newspaper sales. Even Harbaugh, a friend of Rhoderick's, admitted that he'd agreed to write to the paper in order to help his friend out with the scheme. The scheme worked, of course, but when a hoax starts to influence the President of the United States… it may be time to call it a day, the men said.

Snallygaster sightings tapered off after that, with virtually no talk of the monster until the mid-1930s. In Pendleton, West Virginia, The *Pendleton Times* reported in March 1935 that the Snallygaster was terrorizing a family in Monkeytown. The paper said one Kennie Bland was treed by the beast and left "high in the air." Later, the Snallygaster was spotted in Hopewell, where it roared at locals. At the time, according to an essay by Jason Burns, the beast spewed a "poison vapor" wherever it went, preying mostly upon those who were "less than pious."

In Maryland, Charles Main reported a Snallygaster flew over South Mountain in Middletown. A Middletown resident and ice cream entrepreneur, Main claimed he'd spotted the creature in November 1932, when he was returning from Frederick early one morning. The creature flew no more than 25 feet off the ground, with a wingspan of between 12 and 14 feet, throwing out long octopus-like arms occasionally, Main said.

The Evening Sun, in Baltimore, reported that the creature had fallen out of a persimmon tree and gone on a cider bender in High Knob, eventually commandeering a bicycle and peddling its way up into the mountains.

More reports followed in the 1940s, including more in Hopewell, West Virginia, where it attacked a hound dog named "Old Dog Blue." The dog allegedly noticed the beast, according to reports, and started howling to warn the neighborhood, but failed to give chase since he'd been paralyzed by the Snallygaster in a previous attack. People in the town retreated safely to their homes, reports indicate, but not before they saw the cryptid's fiery eyes and its monstrous metallic teeth.

A few years later, it returned to Hopewell, terrorizing the dog population of the town, once again. One dog, who was said to be deaf, didn't hear the Snallygaster's howl, and was killed by the creature. Local women hid in their attics to get away from the beast, but, according to re-tellings, one woman was so scared she fell out of her attic and into the pig's slop barrel, necessitating a rescue by her husband.

It wouldn't be until Hopewell and Monkeytown began installing electric lights in the late 1940s that tales of the Snallygaster would end in West Virginia.

In Maryland, the Snallygaster was reported to have met a tragic end. A Washington County, Maryland moonshiner claimed the Snallygaster had flown over his still and passed out from the fumes. When the bird-lizard fell, it dropped into his 2,500-gallon vat and drowned, only to be destroyed later by revenue agents when they demolished the moonshine operation and its product.

Still, the monster made its way into popular culture. In the 1960s, the Pepsi Company named a drink made up of Mountain Dew and vanilla ice cream, called "The Snallygaster". And in 1976, the *Washington Post* is reported to have funded an expedition to find the creature. Nothing was ever found, though. Even today, it's hard to verify the *Washington Post* actually funded the expedition, and wasn't just joking about it.

Sarcasm in print is really hard.

Creating a museum for a monster

But the story of the Snallygaster is one that should get more attention, the Snallygaster Museum's Cooper said.

"There's the Jersey Devil and the Dwayyo that get more attention," Cooper said. "But I feel like the Snallygaster's story is so much more interesting."

Cooper said she first got interested with the Snallygaster during the COVID-19 pandemic. An emergency room nurse, Cooper said she heard about the story and started learning more and more about it to take her mind off of the pandemic and her work.

She started collecting memorabilia, newspaper articles and artwork of the Snallygaster, then set out to teach people in the area about the cryptid. Whether it was putting up a display in a bar, or giving people private tours of her collection, Cooper said she wanted to build a museum to honor Maryland's dragon. By 2021, she was working on building a barn in her backyard to house her collection.

She said she hopes the museum will bring cryptid lovers and others to the Frederick, Maryland area.

"I think it's definitely something that could be a tourism draw," she said. "I've studied the Flatwoods Monster and they have their own museum. And Mothman draws people to Point Pleasant, West Virginia every year."

She even toured cryptid conventions to talk about her

rediscovery of the Snallygaster. In some cases, she was met with skepticism, a skepticism she felt was due to her ethnicity. Most of the people in the cryptid community she met, she said, were mostly white men.

As a self-described "small Asian woman," she also hopes her presence in the cryptid community will help increase its diversity.

"I want the cryptid community to be open for everybody," she said. "I have a lot of kids in the LGBTQ+ community that come to all of my events, and I hope that they will be able to find an accepting community in the cryptid community."

It's thought that the Snallygaster lives for 20 years and then has a 20 year incubation period before another Snallygaster generation hatches and emerges. Its next life cycle, she said, is thought to start in 2024.

With her museum scheduled to open in 2022, she said she plans on being ready.

The Big Muddy Monster

Documentary, Mural Breathe Life into An Old Legend

A new mural in Murphysboro, Illinois includes images of apples, rivers, the nearby Shawnee National Forest, and a large hairy Bigfoot-like creature.

Known as the Big Muddy Monster, the creature that once subjected those who reported seeing it to ridicule, is now something the town embraces.

In fact, a new documentary, "Creature from Big Muddy", looks at the history of the monster as well as its acceptance by the small town it was said to "terrorize" in the 1970s.

The legend of the Big Muddy Monster started around

midnight on June 25, 1973. Randy Needham and Judy Johnson were in a parked car near the Big Muddy River, hoping to take advantage of a little alone time together, when they noticed a foul smell. As they turned and looked out the window to investigate, they saw a 7-foot monster staring back at them.

Covered in white hair and mud, the creature looked like a cousin to the famed Bigfoot monster. With glowing red eyes and yellow teeth, the creature scared the adults enough to make them leave the area and file a police report.

Police investigated the next day and found what appeared to be large narrow footprints.

Later that day, Randy Creath and Cheryl Ray reported seeing the creature on Cheryl's parents farm. Police reports said the couple got an up-close look at the creature.

"Both Randy and Cheryl watched and observed a large creature walk out of the patch of trees near the edge of the yard and then turn around and walk back into the field," the police report said. "The creature was described as being 7 to 8 feet tall, weighing 300 to 350 pounds, pale dirty white, or cream colored, and standing on two feet. Creath stated that he walked toward it and got approximately 30 to 40 feet from it. Creath also stated that it had a musky odor to it."

The multiple sightings made Police Chief Toby Burger's mind up – he decided to hunt the creature down. Taking a posse of men and search dogs, he tracked the monster to an abandoned barn. But as they approached the edge of the barn, the dogs stopped barking and refused to go inside. The investigators went in, but failed to find the creature or any evidence of it being there.

Eventually, the sightings tapered off until 1988, when a salvage yard owner, his employee, his wife and his mother were terrorized by something at his salvage yard. The shop owner said he and his employee spotted the creature and shot it, only to have it turn on them. They took refuge in the yard's metal office space, as the creature banged on the walls for more than a half hour.

All of the encounters, as well as several theories about what the Big Muddy Monster could be — including a hoax — are explored in the 2021 documentary. Joe Tuly, the film's writer and director said he wanted to look at all sides of the story.

"It's a unique story," Tuly said. "Not only did people claim to see something, but it was investigated by the police and documented… I'm not out to prove or disprove the stories at all. I just love the stories and want to explore them."

For him, the fact the story is equally possible to be true and not true is what sets it apart. Located just a few miles from the Shawnee National Forest, the area has plenty of swampland, caves and other areas where something that big could hide, he said, and the area is also home to any number of people who claim to know the person or persons responsible for the hoax.

Chad Lewis, a paranormal and cryptid investigator, wrote the book on the Big Muddy Monster — "The Big

Muddy Monster: Legends, Sightings and Other Strange Encounters" — with coauthors Kevin Lee Nelson and Noah Voss. Once the book came out, he said, interest in the monster picked up. He and Nelson also took part in the documentary. Being in the film allowed him to see the monster in a new light, he said.

"The main thing I took away from this project was the severe and life-changing effects that were caused by encountering this beast," he said. "Witness after witness commented on how powerful this event was in shaping the rest of their lives. Some wanted nothing to do with the story; they wanted to put the incident as far behind them as they could. Others were propelled to dig deeper into the mystery in order to help understand what actually happened to them. For some, even 40 plus years later, the event continued to terrorize and perplex them."

Even now, the monster has begun to change the town of Murphysboro.

"Of course sightings of the beast continue to this day and the town is really beginning to embrace the legend," Lewis said. "The town has a new mural of the beast, they are building a statue of it, they have named a road after it, and local businesses are incorporating it into their names."

The town even has a Big Muddy Brew Fest. Started 12 years ago by the Friends of Murphysboro, the festival raises money to fund projects in the area like dog parks and splash pads. Funds raised by the festival go toward other projects designed to better the town and the surrounding area, the group said.

While the Big Muddy Monster may have once terrorized the residents of Murphysboro, town residents, like residents of many other communities across the country, have come to embrace the creature for what he represents - an unknown lurking in the woods that people want to know more about.

The Flatwoods Monster

West Virginia's Other Visitor Launches a Career and Helps a Modern Company

In the early 1950s, America was gripped with UFO fever. Even in rural West Virginia, strange sights and eerie encounters leapt off the pages of local newspapers and into the annals of the paranormal forever.

Such was the case of the Flatwoods Monster.

On Sept. 12, 1952, the May brothers, Ed, 13, and Freddie, 12, were playing with their friend Tommy Hyer, in the playground near their school near Flatwoods, West Virginia. Near dusk, they saw a pulsing red light shoot across the sky toward the farm of a neighbor, G. Bailey Fisher.

Passing the May home, the boys told Ed and Freddie's mother, Kathleen May, what they had seen. She, in turn, called on West Virginia National Guardsman Eugene Lemon to go to the Fisher farm with them to investigate. Two other neighbor children, Neil Nunley and Ronnie Shaver, as well as the family dog, Richie, joined them.

When the group reached the top of the hill between their house and Fisher's farm, they found their pulsing red light. Lemon reported that he aimed a flashlight in the light's direction and glimpsed a tall "man-like figure with a round, red face surrounded by a pointed hood-like shape."

Kathleen described the creature as having "small, claw-like hands," clothing-like folds that looked like a metal dress, and a "head that resembled the Ace of Spades." The group said when the figure made a hissing sound and glided toward them, Lemon screamed and dropped his flashlight, prompting the whole group to flee in terror.

According to local newspaper reports, despite a heavy mist, the group said they could make out the monster, hovering above the ground, spewing gas and smoke. Later, group's members said they experienced throat irritation, vomiting, and nausea that lasted for days. Many people attributed the symptoms to hysteria, but others noted that the symptoms were also indications of exposure to mustard gas.

Around that same time on the same day, the local sheriff and a deputy were sent to investigate reports of a crashed aircraft in the same area. The two law enforcement officers said they didn't see, hear or smell anything out of the ordinary there.

About an hour after the event however, A. Lee Stewart, Jr., co-publisher of the *Braxton Democrat*, said he and several other men went to the May's house, armed with shotguns, intent on returning to the site of the encounter. The witnesses, he said, were terrified.

"Those people were the most scared people I had ever seen," he told the *Charleston Gazette*. "People don't make up that kind of a story that quickly."

Stewart and his group described the site as having a foul stench, and that the area seemed hotter than normal.

State police laughed the report off, attributing it to hysteria.

Naturally, newspapers across the country picked up the story, as did radio stations. Calls started coming in to the May family from all over the country asking about the monster. And people came from all over to investigate. A minister from Brooklyn came to question the Mays, while a Pittsburgh paper sent a special reporter. Writers Gray Barker and Ivan T. Sanderson, who specialized in UFOs, came to look into the event

It even drew the attention of the U. S. Air Force.

In March of 1952, the Air Force began an investigation into UFOs and whether or not they were a threat to national security. Known as "Project Blue Book," it was the third federal program to look into UFOs, the first being "Project Sign in 1947," followed by "Project Grudge" in 1948, the goal of which mainly seemed to be a way to show that UFOs didn't exist.

Headquartered at Wright-Patterson Air Force Base in Dayton, Ohio, Project Blue Book was initially directed by Captain Edward Ruppelt, with consultations and investigations handled by Dr. J. Allen Hynek.

Hynek was the director at The Ohio State University's McMillion Observatory. At the time, the 37-year-old professor was a skeptic— an astronomer who could suss out whether something in the sky was a planet, asteroid or other astronomical phenomena. After a meeting with the Air Force, he joined Project Sign, investigating 237 cases over the course of a year.

At the end of Project Sign's duration, Hynek said about 32 percent of the incidents were attributable to astronomical phenomena, while another 35 percent could be explained as being balloons, rockets, flares or birds. Of the remaining 33 percent, 13 percent didn't offer enough evidence to yield an explanation, he said.

If you're not doing the math in your head, that means Hynek found that 20 percent couldn't be explained.

The next year, in 1948, the Air Force started Project Grudge. Because the pretense of the study seemed to be that UFOs couldn't exist, Hynek wasn't asked to investigate any of the incidents. When Project Grudge's report was released, not surprisingly, it found that the UFO phenomena resulted from mass hysteria, deliberate hoaxes, mental illness or naturally attributable objects. The subject, the study said, didn't warrant any further investigation.

But of course, the Air Force DID do further investigation.

Project Blue Book started as a systematic scientific investigation of continued UFO reports. Over the course of the project's 17-year duration, the team, and Hynek would investigate 12,618 UFO reports. In the end, they concluded that most of them were natural phenomena like clouds, stars or aircraft. A number of them were attributed to flights of then-secret reconnaissance planes like the U-2 and A-12. But 701 of the reports were classified as unexplainable — nearly 6 percent.

Hynek was called to investigate the Flatwoods sighting along with Air Force investigators. They determined that what the group saw that night in the woods was a giant horned owl. It was one of the first investigations with Project Blue Book, a project that would become his life's work and change his views.

In later years, Hynek went from being a skeptic to a believer. His field work, and his interviews with witnesses, led him to believe that the witnesses truly felt they had seen something.

"Their standing in the community, their lack of motive for perpetration of a hoax, their own puzzlement at the turn of events they believe they witnessed, and often their great reluctance to speak of the experience, all lend a subjective reality to their UFO experience," he wrote later in his 1977 book, "The Hynek UFO Report."

But the Flatwoods Monster remains a legend, drawing attention to the area, and giving rise to the Braxton County Monster Festival to celebrate the legendary visitor.

While most reports say that the May family's experience was the only sighting of the Flatwoods Monster, according to Visit Braxton, the city's tourism website, there were several more.

Not long before the May's reported their encounter, Mrs. Audra Harper said she saw the monster while she walked through the woods behind her home near Heaters, W.V., about five miles north of Flatwoods. Harper said she and a friend were taking a shortcut through the forest to a nearby store when they noticed a ball of fire on a hill they were passing. Initially ignoring it, the two walked on. When Harper glanced back at the fire it had been replaced with a tall, dark silhouette of a man-shaped figure. It was enough to scare Harper and her friend into running away and hiding in the rocks and boulders nearby, the woman said.

The day after the May's experience, another family, George and Edith Snitowsky and their 18-month-old son, reported driving through Strange Creek, about 20 miles south of Flatwoods, when their car died. George said he tried to restart the car, but had no luck. As they were debating what to do, the couple said they smelled a sulfurous smell that made the baby cry. According to their report, a bright light filled the darkness and a 10-foot-tall creature appeared to float in front of their car. The creature was identical to the creature the May's said they saw, except without the spade-shaped hood.

The Snitowskys said the creature then dragged its

lizard-like hand across the hood of their car and drifted away into the woods. As soon as it was gone, the couple said, the car started and they drove away.

While no other further sightings of the monster have been reported, Flatwoods has embraced its paranormal reputation as a tourist draw with ghost towns, haunted homes and Bigfoot sighting areas located around the museum. In addition to paranormal tours, the area has The Spot, a local establishment serving up alien-themed subs amidst monster-themed decor, ensuring that if you can't see a monster, at least you can eat one.

The resulting legend has also helped save a West Virginia business.

In 2020, the COVID-19 pandemic shuttered the 100-year-old glass-blowing company Blenko Glass, renowned for its handblown post-modern glass pieces in Milton, West Virginia. But in October 2020, at the urging of younger staff members, the company presented for sale a one-time only piece by West Virginia artist Liz Pavlovic representing the Flatwoods Monster.

"This cryptid thing, some folks came presenting to us that there are a whole lot of these folks who love this (cryptid) stuff," Dean Six, vice president of Blenko, said. "Their argument was that the Mothman Festival up in Point Pleasant (W.V.) drew immense crowds, probably more than any other festival in West Virginia... So there's this big arrow pointing toward the fact that these things are popular... and they are easier to market because they (cryptid aficionados) are all hanging out in the same places, talking about the same things at these different events."

Working with Pavlovic, Blenko created a Flatwood Monster figure: a two-piece glass sculpture with a green body topped by a red, spade-shaped head complete with glowing yellow eyes. A cryptid fan herself, Pavlovic said she designed the piece with some of Blenko's other pieces in mind and a nod to cryptid lovers everywhere.

"We obviously hoped that it would do well," she said. "I thought people would enjoy it and I know people are into the Flatwoods Monster, but I didn't expect it to be quite as popular as it was."

Initially, Blenko offered only 100 pieces of the statue for sale over a two-week period. Instead, they sold more than 800 of the statues. Glass blowing artists were making the monster figures day and night, Six said. The piece's popularity, he said, along with a few other pivots the glass-blowing company undertook during the pandemic, helped to ensure the company would survive the resulting economic downturn.

"It was one piece of a reasonably complex path to change what we do that has taken us from hanging on at the margins to being successful and anticipating years of future business," Six said. "I would say one of the things Flatwoods Monster did for us as a company is it convinced us that we don't have to keep playing to the same core audience."

The company has plans to release other cryptid statues, including West Virginia's Mothman, as well as suncatchers of Mothman and Bigfoot.

Since their limited release, the Flatwoods Monster pieces have increased in value, Pavlovic said, noting that one recently sold online for nearly $800.

Six said he's eagerly anticipating the rest of the cryptid collection.

"I didn't buy one (of the Flatwoods Monster figures) and usually I don't regret not taking home a piece," he said. "But now, they're kind of like bitcoin or something. I look forward to the Bigfoot one, which is next and then after that, this crazy little Mothman fellow. It's all very interesting."

Iowa's Van Meter Visitor

Visiting the Van Meter Visitor

More than 100 years ago, a winged specter terrified the residents of Van Meter, Iowa. Renewed interest in the beast has brought television crews, documentarians, paranormal experts and festival goers to the sleepy town.

Called the Van Meter Visitor, the pterodactyl-looking creature first appeared in the small rural town in 1903.

According to legend, over the course of five nights in September and October of that year, several of Van Meter's most upstanding citizens reported seeing a half-human, halfanimal creature with enormous bat-like wings fly above the city.

Multiple people reported seeing the nearly nine-foot-tall creature. It not only flew overhead, jumping from rooftop to rooftop at incredible speeds, but it released, they said, a horrendous "memory erasing" odor and shot bolts of light from a horn on its forehead. Bullets, the legend says, didn't hurt it.

On the first night, witnesses said it was flying across building tops. The next evening it was spotted by the town doctor and a bank cashier. On the third night, a man said he saw it perched atop a telephone pole, while another said it looked like a monster hopping like a kangaroo, and a third, the local high school teacher, likening it to a devil. One of the townspeople, Clarence Dunn, an eye witness to the creature's visits, took a plaster cast of the three-toed footprint it left behind.

These weren't just the town drunk, or some passing stranger. These witnesses were some of the most prominent people in town - the implement dealer who said he shot at it; the town doctor and bank cashier Peter Dunn; and the owner of the local hardware store, O.V. White were among them.

In an attempt to get rid of the beast, the townsfolk banded together to find it. Pitchforks and torches in hand, they followed it to an abandoned coal mine near an old brickyard where they heard noises.

"Presently the noise opened up again, as though Satan and a regiment of imps were coming forth for battle," an Oct.3, 1903 article from the Des Moines Daily News said.

Emerging from the cave were two creatures, one larger and one smaller. In a flash of light, and leaving behind an odor that left those in attendance stunned, the two creatures flew away to escape the crowd. The next morning, however, the creatures returned to find that the town's men had gathered with weapons to get rid of them.

"The reception they received would have sunk the Spanish fleet, but aside from unearthly noise and peculiar odor they did not seem to mind it, but slowly descended the shaft of the old mine," the article said.

Once they descended into the mine, the men got to work, sealing the creatures inside the mine forever. Or so the story goes.

That morning, a legend was born - one that continues to this day.

Chad Lewis, noted paranormal researcher and author, wrote about the incident with co-authors Noah Voss and Kevin Lee Nelson in 2013 in "The Van Meter Visitor (A True & Mysterious Encounter with the Unknown)". People still report seeing the creature, he said.

In the 1980s, a man who had just moved to the area, oblivious to the legend, was walking near the coal mine and reportedly saw a 5-foot-long bat-like creature fly over his head, Lewis said. Then in the 2000s, another man told Lewis that he and his family were driving home to Van Meter when they spotted what appeared to be a giant bird-like creature dead on the side of the road. When the man went back to investigate, he said, the creature was gone.

And around 2006, Lewis said, a pastor waiting for a friend in Colfax, Iowa, spotted what he thought was a dragon in the sky. When he returned home, he googled "Iowa dragon," and came across a picture of what he had spotted – the Van Meter Visitor. Later, in 2014, a couple camping in Iowa City reported an encounter with a giant bird, Lewis said.

And finally, in 2020, in Boone, Iowa, someone reported seeing another giant bird.

"When it flapped its huge wings, all I could see was light, dark, light dark. And it was a huge whoosh, whoosh, whoosh, that I heard," the witness reported.

Lewis said that when he and his co-authors came to investigate the creature, it wasn't a big deal, but since then the draw of the creature has grown.

In fact, the Van Meter Visitor Festival is a yearly draw, bringing in 300 to 500 people, said Rachel Backstrom, a member of the festival organizing committee.

"The legend seems to get more popular every year," she said. "It is probably one of the bigger tourist events for Van Meter, but Van Meter doesn't have a huge tourism industry. The Iowa Veterans Cemetery is probably the town's biggest draw."

The legend has a mixed reception in the town,

Backstrom said.

"There are many people who think it is a fun and interesting legend and enjoy the town history," she said. "Others think it was a complete hoax. It is definitely not as big as Mothman. The legend had been mostly forgotten until Chad, Kevin and Noah started researching their book."

Since the book's release and the beginning of the festival, she said, the legend has gained even more ground outside of Van Meter, including attention from two television shows and a couple of documentary crews.

Still, Lewis said, his research into the creature has left him unsure of what exactly happened over those five nights in 1903.

"I can honestly say that after poring over countless records, interviewing residents, unearthing local history and touring the sites of the original encounters, I am still as puzzled today as the people of Van Meter were back in 1903," Lewis said. "When I first began researching this case, I was convinced that it would turn out to be nothing more than some sort of twisted hoax, yet as I made my way through months of research, the idea of the monster being some sort of prank or joke quickly eroded away."

For Lewis, maybe not knowing is the best result.

"In today's world, where we crave answers for everything and increasingly disregard gray areas in pursuit of black and white certainties, the space for mystery and the unexplained is perpetually shrinking," he said. "I have found peace in knowing that I may never discover what happened in Van Meter during that fateful week of 1903, and perhaps I am not meant to. Perhaps the answer is not nearly as important as the act of seeking it out."

Indrid Cold

The Smiling Man and Ties to High Strangeness in West Virginia

Things always seem mysterious on chilly fall nights in the country.

That was certainly the case in rural West Virginia in the heyday of extraterrestrial encounters. A chance meeting between a sewing machine salesman and a "grinning man" would not only affect the lives of a local family for decades, but affect the legend and lore of paranormal research and alien encounters for years after.

It was a cold November night in 1966 in West Virginia, and sewing machine salesman Woodrow Derenberger was making his way back home to Mineral Wells from a business trip to Marietta, Ohio - about 21 miles away from the city in the northeastern corner of the state. After hearing a noise in the back of his truck, Derenberger pulled over to adjust a sewing machine. When he got back on the road, he noticed lights directly ahead of him.

Thinking the lights were police officers, he stopped, only to discover the lights didn't belong to a car at all. The lights, he told authorities, belonged to a spaceship

Normally, the story would end here - Man sees alien spaceship. Man watches alien spaceship fly away. Man reports alien spaceship to authorities. But in Derenberger's encounter, not only did the story not stop there, but it continued for years.

Naturally, Derenberger reported his encounter to the Parkersburg police. By the next day, the media frenzy surrounding the story took off. Derenberger agreed to be interviewed on live television on WTAP. Taking part in the interview were members of the state police, representatives of the Wood County Airport, the Parkersburg Police and a representative from the Wright Patterson Air Force base in Dayton, Ohio. For 30 minutes, the men peppered Derenberger with questions about the strange encounter.

What Derenberger reported was an aircraft that looked like a "kerosene lamp chimney." A "man" stepped out of the aircraft and approached his truck, he told the men.

"He looked perfectly natural and normal as any human being," Derenberger told Ronald Mains, during the WTAP-TV interview the day after the encounter. "His face looked like he had a good tan, a deep sun tan. He was not too dark, but it was just like he had been out in the sun a lot and had a good tan. His hair was combed straight back, and it was a dark brown and he seemed to have a good thick head of hair. His eyebrows, his face, his features were very normal. I don't believe that he looked any different from any other man that you would meet on the street."

But he wasn't normal, Derenberger said. He had a large grin, and kept his arms folded with his hands up under his armpits. And though he "spoke" to Derenberger, his smile never moved. He communicated, Derenberger said, telepathically. "He asked me to roll down the window on my right-hand side of my truck and I done what he asked," Derenberger said during the interview.

"And this man stood there, and he first asked me what I was called, and I know he meant my name and I told him my name and he asked me, he said, 'Why are you frightened?' He said, 'Don't be frightened, we wish you no harm'. He said, 'We mean you no harm. We wish you only happiness,' and I told him my name and when I told him my name, he said he was called 'Cold'." Derenberger told interviewers.

It was Derenberger's, and the world's, introduction to the entity known as "Indrid Cold."

After the interview aired, however, others came forward with claims they had also seen a figure matching Derenberger's description of Indrid Cold. One man reported that a man matching Indrid Cold's description tried to flag him down, but he was too afraid to stop.

Other people claimed to see lights and "fluttering vehicles" on the road where Derenberger said he talked to Cold. And several witnesses reported they had seen Derenberger stopped on the road talking to a man on the same road.

For the next three weeks, newspapers in the area ran stories about the mysterious Indrid Cold.

News coverage eventually died down, but Cold's visits with Derenberger continued. The strange grinning man visited him several times over the course of the next month. Eventually, Derenberger's family said they too had seen Cold and other strange things. In fact, the family reported they continued to receive visits from Cold for decades.

"More than anything, the case of Indrid Cold is a puzzle," said Zelia Edgar, a paranormal researcher who specializes in UFO investigations and Indrid Cold. "It involved the story of a, by all accounts, normal man… whose life went off the rails as soon as he claimed contact with a non-human intelligence. His case falls squarely into the contactee movement — those who believe that they have made such contact with non-human intelligence — and, like many contactees, it seems likely that he believed his initial story. However, also like many contactees, his later claims are rife with confabulation."

Derenberger claimed the contact with Cold extended so far as going on off-planet trips with him to Cold's home planet of Lanulos, a utopian society of cheerful nudists, in the galaxy of Ganymede.

"His family has come forward to confirm that, after his initial encounter, strange people would visit the house," Edgar said. "However Derenberger would not claim that these people were affiliated with Indrid Cold; he believed that they had been sent by some shady government organization or, for reasons unknown, the Mafia."

Naturally, the media attention given to the story brought locals to Derenberger's house, hoping to get a glimpse of Cold. The attention, as well as the scorn and ridicule directed at him, led Derenberger to seek medical attention. His physician gave him a clean bill of health, and found no evidence of chemical imbalance or disruption.

Although he wrote a book about his visits, "Visitors from Lanulos," nothing good came from Derenberger's recounting his encounter. In fact, it didn't just negatively affect him, but it affected his family and his friends as well. The family received years of harassing phone calls and blamed lost jobs and friends on Derenberger's tales of Indrid Cold. Derenberger suffered from painful headaches and depression, and eventually his wife divorced him. Derenberger moved away from the area to escape his notoriety.

After years of living elsewhere, Derenberger moved back to the Mineral Wells area before his death in 1990 at the age of 74 – more than two decades years after Indrid Cold supposedly pulled him over on the highway. While he never recanted his statement, he never spoke of them again either.

Since then, Derenberger's account has lingered,

propelling Indrid Cold into the realm of rural myths and legends as well as into tales of the creepy and unknown. After Derenberger spoke to John Keel, the author of "The Mothman Prophecies," the legend of Indrid Cold was linked to Mothman – even so far as appearing in the 2002 "The Mothman Prophecies" movies. Keel wrote that the "high strangeness" that surrounds Point Pleasant, West Virginia, may link all of the paranormal events that happened in the area at that time, Edgar said.

For it wasn't just that Mothman haunted Point Pleasant for 13 months, Edgar said, but that at the same time people were reporting encounters with Indrid Cold, as well as poltergeist activity, UFOs, apparitions and a wide spectrum of other paranormal events.

Mothman was sighted in Point Pleasant between November 15, 1966, to December 15, 1967. Derenberger encountered Cold on November 2, 1966. Prior to that, two teenagers in Elizabeth, New Jersey, reported they saw a hulking "grinning man". That same day, four miles north, a police officer and his wife saw what they described as a blurry, white light as big as a car near an explosive factory, fly over the hills and vanish. Two other police officers, on the other side of the same hill, reported seeing the same thing.

For Derenberger, the sighting wasn't a blessing.

"It wasn't as simple as seeing a UFO and moving on," Edgar said. "His life was changed — and for the worse. After claiming contact with Indrid Cold, his marriage developed problems, finally ending in divorce. He became obsessed with the story he had woven about the planet Lanulos...

Regardless of the truth or falsity of his experiences, regardless of how much or how little he believed, he really became ensnared by Cold."

The story of Derenberger and Cold shows how much a paranormal encounter can affect someone's life, Edgar said.

"The greatest takeaway from the legend of Indrid Cold is how someone's life can be altered dramatically by something we don't understand," she said. "I personally find it likely that Derenberger believed his initial experiences. That isn't to say that an actual, physical lantern-shaped craft landed, and an entity named Cold got out and talked to the guy, but that a normal man experienced something, possibly the same vague 'something' that was responsible for the many UFO sightings, poltergeist manifestations, and creature appearances in the area... the effect remains that a person's life was drastically altered by an unknown, and that, if it could happen to him, it could really happen to anyone."

In fact, his daughter believes it's still happening to her.

In the paranormal investigation series "Hellier," researchers Greg and Dana Newkirk are searching for hobgoblins in Hellier, Kentuck. In the second season of the series, their search takes them to the nursing home where Taunia Derenberger, Woody Derenberer's daughter, lives.

Throughout their interview with her, she maintains that she still receives regular visits from Cold's family. Taunia Derenberger wrote "Beyond Lanulos: Our Fifty Years with Indrid Cold" documenting the family's history with the "smiling man."

Despite the books and reports of visits, the truth of what exactly happened is still unknown.

With only the Derenbergers word to go on, it's difficult to tell if it really happened, said Brian Dunning, editor of Skeptoid Magazine, but it's clear Derenberger gained nothing from coming forward.

"Who knows what actually happened to Derenberger on that strange night," Dunning said. "Derenberger's story did little for him. His obsession with it cost him his job and his wife. According to Keel, who visited him a year later, they found him 'hiding behind drawn curtains' from what he believed were 'hundreds of UFO believers and skeptics,' saying that 'Indrid Cold and his friends frequently visited the farm, often arriving by automobile, for long, friendly chats.' He had almost certainly become delusional."

That being said, his initial encounter — coming across a lone stranger on a country backroad — is the basis for many paranormal tales. Dark nights on lonely rural roads will always be a good setting for mysterious encounters, Dunning said.

"Rural areas are always the best place for a creepy tale," he said. "It's dark, there are trees and murky creeks, and you are far from the comforting protection of lights and people."

The Georgia Guidestones

Conspiracy-laden Site Succumbs to Conspiracy-driven Vandalism

On July 6, 2022, around 4 in the morning, an explosion rocked the rural countryside near Elberton, Georgia.

When first responders investigated, they found part of the Georgia Guidestones destroyed. One of the five pillars that made up what was sometimes called the American Stonehenge was damaged, blown up by a bomb. Investigators were stymied. Who would want to damage the mysterious monoliths?

Within a few hours, backhoes had taken down the rest of the granite shrine. Officials said the explosion had left the remaining pillars too unstable. Authorities in Elberton decided not to try to rebuild the mysterious marker.

It was the end of more than 40 years of questions surrounding the towering monument built in secrecy in a rural northern Georgia field. But the Guidestones controversial beginning could have been what toppled them some 40 years later.

From 1980 until that day in July 2022, the Georgia Guidestones were one of the most intriguing and controversial monuments erected in rural America. Standing more than 19 feet tall, the Guidestones consisted of six giant granite slabs weighing more than 237,000 pounds. Arranged in an X shape, the four outer slabs contained messages for current and future generations, each slab holding 10 rules in different languages: Arabic, Chinese, English, Hebrew, Hindi, Russian, Spanish and Swahili. On the capstone was written a simple message - "Let these be Guidestones to an age of reason."

The rules were simple:

1. Maintain humanity under 500,000,000 in perpetual balance with nature.
2. Guide reproduction wisely – improving fitness and diversity.
3. Unite humanity with a living new language.
4. Rule with passion – faith – tradition – and all things with tempered reason.
5. Protect people and nations with fair laws and just courts.
6. Let all nations rule internally resolving external disputes in a world court.
7. Avoid petty laws and useless officials.
8. Balance personal rights with social duties.
9. Prize truth – beauty – love – seeking harmony with the infinite.
10. Be not a cancer on the Earth – Leave room for

nature – Leave room for nature.

Naturally, the monument led some to believe it was part a conspiracy to bring about the "New World Order," among other things.

In fact, at least one candidate for public office - Kandiss Taylor, who ran for governor of Georgia in 2022 - deemed the Guidestones satanic. Getting rid of them was a top priority of her campaign.

"Since my election, the Supreme Court has ruled in favor of THREE of my main platform issues and executive orders (Jesus, Guns, and Babies), and Just like Religious persecution, Gun Control, and abortion, the Georgia Guidestones, a demonic monument that calls for the depopulation of the earth, as well as for the extermination of 7.5 Billion people, has no place in the Christian state of Georgia, or in America for that matter!" Taylor said in a statement (capitalization is hers). "This looks like another Act of God to me. Today, it is another defeat of the devil. Never underestimate the power of Prayer!"

The Guidestones' messages disturbed many in the faith community. Clint Harper, a pastor in Franklin County, took issue with the population guidelines.

"To maintain humanity under 500 million people, that means that this monument that is in Elbert County advocates the killing of 6.5 billion people," he said to Elbert County commissioners in June 2022, as he was advocating for the Guidestones' destruction. In his mind, leaving the stones standing and maintaining the Guidestones on county property was tacit endorsement of the monument's messages.

Since their beginning, they've been somewhat controversial.

The story started in 1979 when a "mysterious stranger" who called himself R. C. Christian came to Elberton searching for someone to design and build the monument. According to Joe Fendley, Sr., president of the Elberton Granite Finishing Company, the grey-haired, suit-wearing Christian admitted that his name was a pseudonym. He also said that he represented a group of conservative Christians. To this day, who he really was and the name of the organization he represented is still unknown, if in fact he ever existed at all.

Regardless, Christian said he chose Elberton because of its abundant supply of granite, its rural location and its mild climate. Some say he came to the area because his ancestors once lived there.

It's important to point out here that Elbert County is one of the biggest granite production areas in the country, and has had active granite quarries since the late 1800s. The town has also done a number of things to draw attention to its main industry, including building a granite museum and building a high school football stadium out of granite which has been listed as an important historic site by the Georgia Trust for Historic Preservation.

Anyway, Christian told city leaders and granite builders that he wanted to build this monument with "wisdom for the ages" in the hope that other small communities would follow suit and do the same.

It's also important to point out that 1979/1980 was during a fairly intense period of the Cold War. Tensions between the U.S. and Russia had been ratcheting up since the mid-70s and the threat of nuclear war was the closest it had been since the end of World War II. While America and the Soviet Union had reached detente in 1971, an investigation in 1976 found that the U.S. had grossly under-estimated the Russian's nuclear arsenal and military strength. Some in the U.S. intelligence community felt that not only did the USSR have the tools to win a nuclear war, but that they could win if it ever came to that.

So… coming up with ideas on how to run a world government following a global disruption? Perfectly normal, right?

Clearly, this was a boon for Fendley and his compatriots in the granite industry. Fendley said that he didn't think Christian was serious and quoted him an outrageous price. When Christian agreed to the price, Fendley put his men to work.

Working with a banker, Wyatt C. Martin, president of Granite City Bank, to purchase a five-acre plot in the middle of a cow pasture nearly equidistant between Elberton and Hartwell, Georgia. Christian said the plot afforded dynamic views of the east and west, and was reportedly "in close proximity to what the Cherokee Indians called 'Al-yeh-li A lo-Hee,' — the center of the world."

Again, it's important to point out that the county owns and maintains that property, but that the farmer that owned the property was given grazing rights for the property around the monument for life. Also, for all intents and purposes, the Cherokee nation extended up into Kentucky and from South Carolina into Alabama. It's not clear whether this 'Center of the World' was an actual designation, or an estimation of what Elbert County leadership wanted it to be.

Once erected, the Guidestones were almost immediately infamous locally, and left many people with the notion there was some nefarious purpose behind them. From shadowy groups trying to oppress the world population to their being some sort of magical manifesto, the stones began to divide the locals. Some even believed it was the landing site for alien spacecraft.

On top of the rules for post-apocalyptic governance, the stones also contained astronomical phenomena. Each of the four upright slabs that formed the X were aligned with the moon's migration during the course of the year. In the Gnomen stone, or the middle pillar, an oblique, eye-level hole pointed upward toward the heavens and was oriented to Polaris, the North Star. In the middle of the stone, was a large slot with a hole cut through it that lined up with the summer and winter solstices. Another hole drilled through the capstone served as a sundial, allowing light to shine on the southern face of the Gnomen stones at noon.

All of this, combined with the unknown identity of "Mr. Christian," led people to speculate on what the meaning of the monuments were and how it came to be placed there.

A small tablet at the foot may give some clues. In addition to listing out all the people involved in the design and construction of the monument (including the companies who had provided labor), as well as all of the monument's special properties, a sentence at the bottom of the tablet says more information about the monument is available at the Elbert County Granite Museum.

Locally, the stones gathered a bit of attention, but it wasn't something that immediately caught on in the paranormal community. The 1970s had seen a resurgence in the Bigfoot phenomenon, and in the 80s, society had moved on to ghosts, goblins and global thermonuclear war thanks to movies such as Poltergeist, Hellraiser and War Games.

While the stones remained a relatively unknown mystery in America, the monument was featured in Time Life books and other publications as one of the mysterious places in the U.S., and it did attract its share of attention. Its controversy was its calling card, and annually, it attracted visitors to the sleepy little town.

I was one of those visitors in 2012. Not only did I visit the stones, but my traveling companion and I visited the property records office as well. Like many small-town property records offices, plat books were laid out in the open and available for viewing. The property that the Guidestones were located on had changed hands in 1980 for $10.

Hardly the price someone would charge if they wanted to take advantage of a millionaire.

The stones did draw in tourists though.

Christopher Kubas, the executive vice president of the Elberton Granite Association, said the stones brought in about 20,000 visitors a year.

"I've met people from Australia, from China, from all over the world here at these Guidestones," Kubas said.

Still, the stones didn't draw the attention that something like a Stanley Hotel, Eastern State Penitentiary or the Winchester House would bring in. Just in comparison, the Winchester House in California has brought in on average more than 121,000 people per year to visit its weird rambling halls and purported paranormal architectural elements. Some articles would emerge about the Guidestones periodically, like a 2009 piece in Wired Magazine that wrote the stones off as hippie, New Age ideology coupled with Koch-ian eugenics and conservative world-building mantras.

All that changed, however, during Taylor's candidacy.

Taylor said the entire site was "satanic" and had as one of her campaign planks a pledge to destroy it via executive order. While Taylor came in third, the attention her campaign brought to the monuments was more venomous than touristy.

Evangelical Christians and fringe conspiracy theorists latched on to the Guidestones as evidence of everything from the Lizard people controlling the Democrats to a portal to hell.

Elberton Mayor Daniel Graves said the idea of a Satanic monument in his staunchly conservative and religiously observant area doesn't make sense. Neither did the monument's destruction, he said.

"Our view of righteousness is not an Almighty God that needs zealots to do his dirty work and destruction," Graves said.

On the morning of July 6, however, all of that came to an end with an explosion and a Camaro.

The explosion rocked the area. Pieces of the monument were found hundreds of feet away. When they arrived, local and state police found evidence of a bomb and one pillar mostly destroyed.

The size and force of the blast was massive. While it only destroyed one of the pillars, the bomb was clearly intended to take out more, said Northern Circuit District Attorney Parks White, who declared the bombing an act of "domestic terrorism."

"The power of this device they detonated was enormous," White said. "The Guidestones are officially owned by the governing authority of Elbert County, and any structure open to the public and owned by a subdivision of the state is considered a public building."

If an arrest is made, and someone is convicted of domestic terrorism, the crime carries a possible sentence of a minimum 20 years in prison without the possibility of parole.

Strange Female Legends

Maidens in Myth

Bigfoot. Mothman. Little Green Men. The VanMeter Visitor.

What do they all have in common? Well, aside from being rural monsters, they're all, supposedly, men.

Let's face it, there aren't really that many female legends.

In a world dominated by male figures, finding a good female cryptid role-model is hard. From Lizardman to Bunnyman to Loveland's Frogman and Michigan's Dogman, the cryptid world is definitely a sausage fest.

In rural myths and legends, however, women may be monsters out to steal your children or find their dead husbands. Certainly, they all fall into two very distinct categories - witches and spirits.

Witches

The Bell Witch

Probably the most well-known rural myth witch is the Bell Witch.

The Bell Witch has been called America's greatest ghost story. Starting in the early 19th century, reports of a spirit haunting a family in Robertson County, Tennessee drew skepticism and curiosity.

John Bell was born in Halifax County, North Carolina in 1750. In 1782, Bell married Lucy Williams, the daughter of a prominent North Carolina farmer. John and Lucy settled in her home county of Edgecomb, and began their family. Eventually, with the Bell family consisted of nine children on a 1,000-acre farm on the Red River in Robertson County, Tennessee.

Legend says that on a sunny day in 1817, John Bell was inspecting his corn field when he saw a strange animal with the body of a dog and the head of a rabbit. Shocked, Bell fired at the animal several times, only to watch it vanish.

While Bell thought nothing more of the incident, it was the beginning of four years of incidents at the Bell farm. The "haunting" started that night when the family heard what sounded like someone beating on the outside walls of their log home.

The children also started to see strange creatures around the property. Most of the activity centered around the Bell daughter Betsy. She and her brothers began to hear knocking on doors and windows, wings flapping against ceilings and rats gnawing on bedposts. Later, they reported hearing the sounds of choking and strangling, as well as chains dragging and objects hitting the floor.

Activity in and around the house continued to increase - the children reported being physically abused with their hair being pulled as well as being pinched and struck. In one instance, the witch recited the sermons of two separate ministers despite them having been given at the same time more than 12 miles apart.

When Betsy got engaged to her childhood sweetheart Joshua Gardner, the witch relentlessly abused her - ruthlessly taunting her and physically abusing her through slaps and hair pulling. As a result, Betsy called off the marriage, while remaining attached to Joshua. But the witch's attacks continued. The strain of it was so hard on Betsy that she became prone to fainting spells, often appearing exhausted and lifeless.

When Betsy called off the engagement, the witch turned her attention to John Bell. Since the episodes with the witch began, Bell had been suffering from twitching in his face, as well as difficulty swallowing. With time, these conditions grew worse. By the fall of 1820, more than three years after the first incident, Bell was so sick, he was confined to the house where the witch mercilessly tormented him. On the morning of December 19, 1820, John Bell slipped into a coma and died the next day. Upon his death, the Bell family found a vial of black liquid in a cupboard. One of Bell's sons sprinkled drops of the concoction on the family's pet cat's tongue.

Immediately, the cat jumped into the air, flipped and died before it hit the floor. Family members said the witch was heard to say, "I gave Ol' Jack (her nickname for John Bell) a big dose of that last night, which fixed him!"

His son tossed the vial into the fireplace where it burst into flames that shot up the chimney.

Being a prominent citizen of Tennessee, John Bell's funeral was one of the largest ever held in Robertson County. Mourners came from miles to pay their respects, while three preachers - two Methodist and one Baptist - eulogized him. Crowd members reported hearing the Bell Witch laughing and singing a song about a bottle of brandy. After Bell's death, the family's torment stopped, as if the witch had accomplished what it set out to do.

After John Bell's death, the incidents began to dissipate. Betsy married her former school teacher, Richard Powell, and the two moved to Mississippi.

Since then, the story has attracted attention from ghost hunters, skeptics, supernaturalists, and others. The witch promised to return to Lucy Bell in 1828, and to John Bell's descendants in 1938. Many have reported unexplained activity in and around the Bell farm in Adams, Tennessee, and at the now famous Bell Witch Cave, which still draws tourists and ghost hunters to the area. The Bell Witch has been the subject of numerous books, documentaries and movies. While the witch has promised that she's done with the Bell family, tales of her high jinx continue to this day.

Hanna Cranna's Ghost

Another rural witch, Hannah Cranna, in Monroe, Connecticut, is reportedly haunted the cemetery there where she is buried. From time to time, residents of the 20,000 person town say the ghost of a woman will appear in the middle of Spring Hill Road, next Gregory's Four Corners Burial Ground where her body is buried. Her appearance causes those who see her to lose control of their car, and sometimes their life.

When she was alive, Hannah Cranna was Hannah Hovey. Born in 1783, Hannah married Capt. Joseph Hovey, who was much older than her. His death was the beginning of Hannah's reputation as the "Wicked Witch of Monroe."

According to legends, Capt. Hovey went out for a simple walk one night near the couple's home off Cutler's Farm Road. Despite knowing the road well, he somehow managed to fall off the side of the road and die. Townspeople in Monroe, naturally, didn't believe it was an unfortunate accident, and started whispering about Hannah. In their minds, she had somehow bewitched him causing him to become confused and tumble to his death.

After his death, it was her behavior that estranged her from the community. While she'd never been too friendly before, she became positively shrewish and loathsome as a widow. Neighbors said she would often expect her neighbors to give her food and firewood. If they didn't, she would use the rumors they'd spread about her against them by threatening to curse them.

One farmer's wife said she was baking pies one day when Hannah asked for one. The wife obliged and gave her a small one. Hannah, however, wanted a larger one. When the wife didn't comply, Hannah "cursed" her, and she was reportedly never able to bake again. Another story goes that a man was fishing for trout on her property without asking her permission. After Hannah cursed him, he was never able to catch another fish.

For years, Hannah lorded over the community helping those who supported her, and making life miserable for those who mocked and ridiculed her.

In 1859, Hannah's rooster, "Old Boreas" died. Many in Monroe were sure that Old Boreas was her "familiar" - an animal used to help in black magic. Once he died, Hannah told a neighbor that she wouldn't last too much longer. With the end nearing, she told her neighbor how she wanted to go.

"My coffin must be carried by hand to the graveyard," she supposedly told them. "And I must be buried before sundown."

She died the next day.

Unfortunately for Hannah, and the townspeople, it was snowing heavily the day of her burial, and locals decided it wasn't all that important to follow her instructions. Instead of carrying her coffin by hand, they decided to pull her casket across the snow on a sled.

As the funeral procession moved from her house

to the cemetery, the coffin came off the sled and slid back to her front door. Even though they tried to pull her on the sled several times, each time, the coffin fell off the sled and slid back to her front door. Eventually, the pall bearers relented and carried her and the coffin to the graveyard. With some trouble, the men were finally able to bury her in the cemetery,... just after sunset. When they returned to her home, they found it engulfed in flames.

Her death then only served to cement her reputation as Hannah Cranna, "The Wicked Witch of Monroe," forever.

Since then, there have been numerous sighting of Hannah on the road next to the cemetery she's buried in. And plenty of people say at least one of the men who was distracted by her ghost drove off the road and crashed into her headstone, dying on impact.

But since her tombstone is located on the top of a hill overlooking the road, the kind of automotive gymnastics that would require... well, that would make Hannah's ghost a pretty powerful witch, wouldn't it?

Spirits
La Mala Hora

There are lots of women ghosts out there. There's not a state out there that doesn't have a tale of a "Crybaby Bridge," where a woman throws her kids off a bridge, and follows them jumping to her death. Women searching for their husbands seem to be wandering all over the place.

But the true terrors, or those female spirits who appear to their victims for no apparent reason other than to do them harm. There are plenty of legends in rural communities of women terrorizing the unsuspecting.

In the deserts of New Mexico, the legend of La Mala Hora haunts the area between Santa Fe and Taos. A dark spirit shaped like a woman dressed either in all black or all white, La Mala Hora appears to anyone, but is particularly fond, it's said, of men. Drivers are told if they see her at a crossroads, or a fork in the road, someone they know, or possibly themselves, will die soon.

Literally translated, La Mala Hora means "the bad hour." Running into this spirit will make any hour the bad hour, but especially so if she's dressed in black.

Dressed in white, she's said to hypnotize travelers who see her. They don't notice that she's floating in the air, or that her toes are backwards, or even the fact that her their flashlights have stopped working and they've lost all sense of direction. Instead they obediently follow wherever she leads, often off the edge of a ravine or in front of a passing car.

When she's dressed in black, La Mala Hora is more aggressive. She'll come at drivers and try to stop them by any means necessary, her long pointed fingers scratching on the windows.

One story repeated often across New Mexico is of a woman named Isabella. In the story, Isabella gets a call from her best friend saying that she needs her to console her as she goes through a divorce. Naturally, Isabella gets in her car and travels the long and lonely road from Santa Fe to Taos. Along the way, she calls her husband who is away on business to tell him that she needs to comfort her friend.

As the moon rises over the deserted road, she reaches a fork in the road and sees a figure dressed all in black standing in the middle of the road. After she slams on her brakes, Isabella turns to look for the woman and realizes she's gone. As she turns back around to drive off, Isabella sees La Mala Hora on her left, scratching at the driver's side window, her glowing red eyes peering into her soul and her wicked grimace breaking out across her face, accentuating her cracked skin.

Terrorized Isabella speeds away without looking back and doesn't strop driving util she reaches her friend's house. After running inside and explaining to her friend what happened, her friend tries her best to comfort her. However, her friend warns her seeing La Holla Mora is an omen.

The next morning, the two friends decided to drive back to Isabella's house. Once they get there they find police cars in the driveway. The police inform them that Isabella's husband is dead - he'd been mugged on his business trip and died at the very moment La Mala Hora had appeared on the road in front of Isabella.

Spearfinger

One of the oldest of these spirit women legends comes from the Great Smoky Mountains National Park.

According to legend, a woman named "Spearfinger" lives in the mountains, going after unsuspecting adults and children to eat their livers.

Spearfinger's real name is U'tlun'ta, or "she had it sharp," referring to her sharp finger on her right hand which gave her the name Spearfinger.

With stone-like skin and a blood-stained mouth, Spearfinger's right hand has a "sharp finger" resembling an obsidian knife, which she uses to cut out her victims livers. Her heart, her only weak spot, is hidden in her right hand, which she keeps tightly closed to protect it.

Legend has it that since she is made of stone, it sounded like rolling thunder when she walked. She crushes rocks and boulders in the ground and her voice bounces off mountains and echos into the valleys and villages, sending birds flying. When birds flocked to the sky, people below said it was a warning that Spearfinger was on the move.

So, according to tales from the Cherokee, Spearfinger built a rock bridge, the "Tree Rock," that reached up into the sky near the "Higher Beings." The gods thought she was too arrogant to try to reach their level, so they struck the bridge down with a bolt of lightning which caused the bridge to crumble down on Spearfinger. The locals say the place she fell is in Blount County, Tennessee, near Nantahala.

Since her fall from grace, Spearfinger has stalked her victims as a shape-shifter. Going after children, she takes on the form of an older lady whom the child knows and doesn't fear. She'll offer to comb their hair to bring them close to her, singing them to sleep before spearing them with her finger and pulling their liver out. Using the fog of the Smoky Mountains, she drifts from one village to the next, looking for fires to guide her to the next victim.

In some cases, she takes the form of those victims in order to lure their parents and other family members to their death. Once they had rescued the "child," and taken them home, Spearfinger waits in the home until the entire family is asleep, at which time she'll creep into the darkness, slit their throats and steal their livers.

If another person comes along while she's luring the children away, she'll change back into stone. In that state, she can't be hurt and arrows don't affect her. And being made of stone, she's strong enough to lift and throw boulders with little effort. It's said she can break them into gravel, stack them into barriers or change them altogether to create even larger boulders that she then rolls down mountains.

In recent years, Spearfinger has been featured on "Mountain Monsters," when a mysterious figure lures one of the monster hunters away. Trapper, Buck, Huckleberry, Jeff, Willy and Wild Bill not only move through the Appalachian Mountains looking for monsters, the team chases seven monsters through the mountains, including Spearfinger.

Women, it's fair to say, oftentimes get the short end of the stick when it comes to life. But in legend, some of the most long-lived of them all are of the fairer sex.

Modern Myths

Meth Hogs, Hobgoblins, "the Watcher" and More

While most rural myths and legends have been around for many years, some, like the Georgia Guidestones, are just emerging. Like other myths and legends, they take on the shape of the concerns facing rural communities. Just as concerns over flying saucers lead to reports of aliens in backwoods farms, more modern rural myths and legends capitalize on our current social fears — drugs, unseen threats and stalkers.

The Meth Hogs of Eastern Kentucky

Southeastern Kentucky has been awash in meth for decades. In towns like Louisa, Ky., deliveries from food banks required police escorts in 2022 because meth addicts have threatened drivers with violence. As other areas of the country have seen a decrease in drug crimes, in areas like Pikeville and Manchester, methamphetamine use has increased over the years.

And with the methamphetamine use comes legends about its effects on local animals.

Starting in 2010, residents in eastern Kentucky reported seeing giant, rage-filled wild hogs destroying cars, homes, and livestock. Some reports have them even attacking people.

Anyone who lives in a rural area in Kentucky, or the southeast for that matter, knows about wild pigs. Feral pigs have been roaming the hills of Eastern Kentucky for decades. According to the Kentucky Department of Fish and Wildlife Resources, wild hogs in the state are an exotic, invasive species brought in by hunters as a game species. Since their introduction into the Kentucky habitats, they have expanded, posing a threat to wildlife, wildlife habitat, natural areas, agriculture and hunting traditions.

The department said wild pigs came to southeastern America in the 1500s, when early European explorers brought domestic pigs with them as livestock. But they allowed the pigs to roam freely, encouraging their spread and establishing them as an invasive species.

Wild pigs are usually black or brown, and can weigh between 75 and 250 pounds. Many have physical traits similar to their Eurasian wild boar ancestors: long coarse hair, broad shoulders, and grizzled coat coloration. Generally, they're harmless unless cornered, and will do what they can to hide away from humans.

But that all started to change, according to legend,

in the early 2000s in Harlan County. People there started reporting enormous, deformed hogs coming into town from the hills.

While no one knows for sure what happened to mutate the animals, most assume, and repeat, that the hogs came upon a "chemical refining business" in Harlan County, in other words, a meth lab.

In one version of the story, the meth lab operator had been throwing whatever he had leftover into a large plastic bottle with "Do Not Drink" on it, as a means of disposing of his production waste. Because wild pigs can't read, it turned out to be an irresistible treat to the creature, who snarfed it down like slop on a farm. In some versions of the tale, the concoction was laced with enough hormone-altering substances to reanimate the pigs latent "wild boar" DNA and change their physiognomy to wild hog.

The first sighting of Meth Hogs happened in the hills of Harlan County in 2005. According to reports, a hunter said he was charged by an enormous hog he estimated to be about 10 feet long, 4 feet high and topping out at about 900 pounds. The hunter said the hog had not one, but two sets of unusually long tusks protruding from unusual angles from its mouth.

Reports said the hog came after the hunter who had to climb a tree to escape the animal attack. The hunter said the hog repeatedly charged the tree, forcing the hunter to shoot at it multiple times. The hunter said that instead of stopping it, the shots just seemed to "piss it off more than anything else."

After a few hours, the hog retreated and eventually wandered off, leaving the hunter with an opportunity to leave the scene in his truck.

Since then, other sightings have been reported throughout Eastern Kentucky. Allegedly, the hogs have been attacking livestock, eating chickens, dogs, and goats. Some residents have even reported hogs dragging off full-grown cows into the woods.

Other reports indicate the Meth Hogs may have killed someone in September 2008. Allegedly, a family of four was camping in the Kentenia State Forest, near Putney, Kentucky in Harlan County. Reports indicate their camp site was discovered by a park ranger. The tent and campsite had been completely destroyed, trampled to the ground and covered in cloven hoof prints. While the ranger found blood and traces of clothing, the family was never found.

Several other disappearances were reported in the years that followed until 2010 when one of the mutant hogs was reportedly killed. Authorities said a trapper was using a foot gripping trap, when he caught one of the creatures. The animal was reportedly furious at being caught, and the trapper said the wild hog tried to chew its own leg off trying to escape. The hunter told reporters it took six shots to the head in order to kill the beast. But, the hunter said, the specimen was only about 400 pounds.

What's even more fascinating, he said, was that the animal's skin was almost impossible to cut open. When he was trying to dress the pig for slaughter, he said, he had to use a chainsaw to cut through the skin to get out the organs. Once he did cut the skin, he said, the smell from inside the animal's body was overpowering. The hunter said it smelled more like "eggs that had been left rotting in the sun," than it did a dead pig.

Other irregularities included fat just under the skin that was laced with a thick web of cartilage. The combination of the cartilage and fat would create a sort of bullet-proof vest, the hunter said, flexible when the animal was moving, but incredibly firm when hit directly.

The hunter also noticed that the hog's internal organs were unusual. He said the creature had two livers, four kidneys and a bevy of lumpy tumors throughout its body. In addition, it had its own version of "meth mouth" with six 8-inch long tusks protruding from its mouth at odd angles and two additional rows of teeth. And if that wasn't bad enough, the creature reportedly had four testicles.

But are the tales real?

Without a doubt, there are tales circulating on the internet about meth hogs. But meth hogs are also characters created on "Squidbillies," a late night AdultSwim cartoon by Jim Fortier and Dave Willis. The series premiered in 2005, and ended after 132 episodes in 2021.

The cartoon series centers around the Cuyler family, a poor family of anthropomorphic hillbilly squids living in the Blue Ridge Mountains. The series revolves around the family and the exploits of its alcoholic father, his teenage son, the mother and grandmother in the family, and Lil, the father's sister who is mostly unconscious throughout the series in a pool of her own vomit.

While there are no police reports of wild hogs ravaging the Harlan County hillsides, there have been official police reports of meth being transported in stuffed pigs.

According to the Osage County Sheriff's Office in Linn, Mo., sheriff's deputies and agents from the U.S. Drug Enforcement Agency seized a stuffed pig containing over a pound of meth. Officials said the seizure was part of a month-long investigation by the Mid-Missouri Drug Task Force and the Osage County Sheriff's Office involving a drug ring with connections to Nevada.

The Hobgoblins of Hellier, Ky.

In 2012, Greg Newkirk, a full-time paranormal investigator and the founder of the Traveling Museum of the Occult and Paranormal, received an email from a man in Hellier, Ky.

Newkirk said the man, Dr. David Christie, claimed that he and his family were being terrorized by creatures coming from the caves behind his house. Christie said the creatures killed his dog and ran after his children. He even sent pictures of the creatures' footprints to Newkirk in emails.

At first, Newkirk corresponded with the man, but eventually, the correspondence stopped. Christie had disappeared. Five years later, Newark and a team of researchers traveled to Hellier, an unincorporated town in Pike County, Kentucky. Their goal was to find Christie and look into whatever it was that had terrorized his family.

Once they arrived, however, they found that no one in the area had ever heard of the doctor. Undaunted, the group continued their investigation, turning their adventure into a two season, 11-episode television series on Amazon Prime.

Along the way, the crew visited the International Paranormal Museum and Research Center in Somerset, Kentucky. They also visited Taunia Derenberger, the daughter of Woody Derenberger, the man who originally reported meeting Ingrid Cold, an alien visitor.

The investigators looked into several theories including secret societies, and conditions in the area that may lead to high rates of mental health issues. But they never found Christie, and they never found the hobgoblins. The tale remains a mystery.

The Watcher

Every old home comes with its own set of problems left by the previous owner. But in one case, the "problem" seems to have been someone tied to the previous owner.

In 2014, Derek and Maria Broaddus moved into their

dream home at 657 Boulevard in Westfield, New Jersey. A home in one of the safest neighborhoods in the state, the house was everything the Broaddus' wanted it to be— their little piece of the American dream.

At least it started out that way.

Three days after they moved in, a letter came in their mailbox. Addressed to "The New Owner", the letter welcomed the family to 657 Boulevard. Then, it took a turn.

"657 Boulevard has been the subject of my family for decades now and as it approaches its 110th birthday, I have been put in charge of watching and waiting for its second coming (...) It is now my time. Do you know the history of the house? Do you know what lies within the walls of 657 Boulevard? Why are you here? I will find out," the letter said.

The letter went on to identify the Broaddus' minivan, their renovation plans, and even some details about the children.

At the bottom, the letter was signed "The Watcher."

At first, of course, Derek alerted the authorities. But after the police investigation into the letters stalled Derek decided to contact the previous owners of 657 Boulevard, the Woods family.

As it turns out, the Woods family had gotten a similar letter about a week before moving out that mentioned someone watching the house from afar. But, since it was the first time they'd received a letter like that in the 23 years they'd lived there, they threw the letter away as a crank.

For the next few weeks, the Broaddus family was more than a bit paranoid. Maria and the children stayed at their previous home while Derek canceled business trips and kept the new house under watch. Throughout the disjointed living arrangement, renovations on the house continued. But Derek noticed some strange happenings at the house, like signs missing from their yard.

Eventually, Maria and the children returned to the house to collect the mail and look after renovations. There, in the mailbox, was another letter.

This letter was addressed to the homeowners by name and noted the changes to the house. In fact, the letter listed the children by birth date and nickname, including asking about one child's preference for sitting on the porch and painting.

"Is she the artist in the family?" the letter's author asked. "All of the windows and doors in 657 Boulevard allow me to watch you and track you as you move through the house. Who am I? I am the Watcher and have been in control of 657 Boulevard for the better part of two decades now. The Woods family turned it over to you. It was their time to move on and kindly sold it when I asked them to."

And if that wasn't creepy enough, things got decidedly worse.

As the Broaddus family decided not to return to the house, they looked to the FBI for help. But with few leads, little evidence and a limited number of suspects, the case stalled. In 2016, just two years after buying the house, the Broaddus' decided to tear the building down and rebuild.

The neighbors' were pleased with the family's decision, but The Watcher?

Not so much.

The next letter from The Watcher was much more threatening in nature. Whoever it was threatened the family with punishment should they follow through with their plan to destroy the house.

"Maybe a car accident. Maybe a fire. Maybe something as simple as a mild illness that never seems to go away but makes you feel sick day after day after day after day after day. Maybe the mysterious death of a pet. Loved ones suddenly die. Planes and cars and bicycles crash. Bones break (…) You wonder who The Watcher is? Turn around idiots."

In 2016, the Broaddus family put the house up for sale. Unfortunately, because of the letters and the rumors about The Watcher, the house didn't sell quickly.

Rumors circulated: was it the next-door neighbors with a perfect view of the home? Was it a nearby couple whom police noted played a video game featuring a character named "the watcher?" Or was it even the Broaddus family themselves?

Three years later, in 2019, the 1905 Dutch Colonial with six bedrooms and four bathrooms sold for $959,360, according to Zillow. The Broaddus family reportedly lost more than half a million dollars on the sale. However, so spooked by the letters, the family was eager to get out. As they did, any answers to who was behind the letters faded away.

However, their loss on the house's property value may have been made up on the Netflix battle for the rights to their story. According to Variety, their story sold to Netflix after a bidding war between it and five other studios. The limited series began production in 2022 starring Naomi Watts and Bobby Cannavale.

The Broaddus' also have filed suit against the previous owners of 657 Boulevard, saying the Woods knew about the Watcher's threatening letters, but did not disclose the information to them prior to selling the house.

In response, the former owners said the Watcher was completely fictitious and that the suit should be dismissed.

The Bunny Man

It sounds like the plot of a 1980s teen horror movie: a man dressed in a bunny suit terrorizes residential neighborhoods near Washington, D.C.

But, in fact, it's real. Well, the fact that there are stories spreading through the area is real, and some of the documented facts surrounding the tales are real too. But it's certainly a tale stranger than any Hollywood Scream Queen flick.

The Bunny Man legend started popping up in Maryland and Virginia in the late 1970s. Although his appearances were infrequent and widespread, they tended to occur in secluded, rural locations. At first, it was just a man in a bunny suit. But soon the legend morphed into a gruesome killer.

The stories started in October 1970. That month, Air Force Academy Cadet Robert Bennett was visiting his uncle in Clifton, Virginia, so he could attend the Air Force-Navy football game. Fairfax County police reported that Bennett and his fiancée were sitting in a car on Guinea Road, across from Bennett's uncle's house, when they saw a man "dressed in a white suit with long bunny ears." The man ran out from behind some nearby bushes shouting, "You're on private property and I have your tag number."

The Bunny Man then threw a wooden-handled hatchet through the right front car window. After hitting the car, the Bunny ran off into the night. Bennett and his fiancée were not injured, police reports indicate.

Police said they retrieved the hatchet, but were

unable to gather any other clues from the scene.

Just two weeks later, the Bunny Man reappeared.

In that incident, the man, again in a rabbit suit with two long ears, appeared again on Guinea Road, just a few houses down from where he was originally spotted. This time, he was standing on the front porch of a newly constructed, unoccupied house. A security guard, Paul Phillips, told police he saw the Bunny Man standing on the front porch and approached him.

"I started talking to him," Phillips told the local newspaper. "That's when he started chopping. 'All you people trespass around here.'"

Phillips said the Bunny Man hit eight gashes in a column on the porch.

"'If you don't get out of here, I'm going to bust you in the head,' he told me," Phillips said.

Phillips said when he walked back to his car to get his gun, the Bunny Man ran off into the woods, taking his long-handled ax with him. Phillips said the man was about 5-foot, 8-inches tall and weighed about 160 pounds. Phillips estimated the man was in his early 20s.

Aside from the Donnie Darko vibes, the original reports initially seemed fairly harmless. Within a few years, however, stories started emerging about the Bunny Man chasing kids through the woods with a hatchet. Then, it was reported that children saw him eating bunnies. Soon after, stories started circulating that the Bunny Man caught two children spying on him in his hideout under a bridge, and killed them, leaving their bodies hanging from the bridge as a sign to others.

The locals said the Bunny Man originated in 1904. According to some reports, inmates from a nearby insane asylum escaped while being transferred to Lorton Prison. One of the escapees, Douglas Grifon, murdered his fellow escapee Marcus Walter. Authorities recovered all of the other inmates except Grifon, who remained at large. It was Grifon, locals said, who became Bunny Man.

The tales are so ingrained in the community of Clifton, Virginia now that the one-lane tunnel bridge on Colchester Road is now identified on Google Maps as Bunny Man Bridge. And it's a popular spot for police stakeouts. Legend says if children hang out at the bridge on Halloween night, Buuny Mann will come after them with a hatchet. Bolstered by appearances on "Scariest Places on Earth," a paranormal reality television show hosted originally by Linda Blair of "The Exorcist", thrill seekers show up each year to the bridge, whom local police have to chase off.

While tales of child murders and a pretty strict rabbit-based diet aren't all that provable, local archivist Brian Conley said that accounts from the 70s of a "Bunny Man" roaming Guinea Road, are backed up by police reports.

That hasn't stopped the surrounding area from taking advantage of the tale though. From Bunnyman

Brewing to Bunny Man merchandise, there's plenty of reminders in the area of what the legend means to local residents.

Blue-eyed Indians

Blue-eyed Indians of North Carolina - a clue to the mystery of the "Lost Colony"

Recent discoveries in North Carolina may lead to answers as to where the Outer Banks famous "Lost Colony" went to, but Native Americans say they've known all along.

In fact, they say, the answer lies in their eyes.

For years reports of blue-eyed Indians in North Carolina were thought to be proof that the Lost Colony wasn't lost, but rescued.

Anyone who has spent time on the North Carolina coast Knows the story of the Lost Colony.

In August 1587, a group of English settlers led by Captain John White, settled on Roanoke Island off the coast of what is now the Outer Banks of North Carolina. Later that year, White, governor of the new colony, decided to sail back to England for a fresh load of supplies.

Upon his arrival, however, a war between England and Spain broke out and Queen Elizabeth I refused to let White return to the New World, ordering him and his ship to battle the Spanish Armada.

It would be three years before White could finally return to Roanoke. But when he arrived, all 115 settlers, along with White's wife, daughter and granddaughter, Virginia Dare, were gone. White could find no trace of the colony or its inhabitants apart from a single word – "Croatoan" – carved into a wooden post.

Since that time, many theories have sprung up about the "Lost Colony" – that they died of starvation or disease; that they were victims of a deadly storm; or that they had all been killed by Native American or Spaniards.

But local Indian tribes say they have proof the colonists survived – their eyes.

Members of the Tuscarora tribe say the tribe took the English settlers in, maybe without their consent, and intermingled with the English women. Many of the resulting children had blue eyes, a trait found in the English, but not in Native Americans.

According to legend told by the Tuscarora, on one of their foraging missions, the tribe took the English women of the Roanoke colony as prisoners and killed most of the men – letting three men and one woman go free because they were afraid of their red and blonde hair. These four went back to Roanoke and were taken in by the Croatoan tribe.

The Croatoan tribe asserts that they took the colonists in.

"My European ancestors were among the first to arrive at the remote barrier islands of what we now call North Carolina's Outer Banks," said Licia Berry. "In the 1500s, the islands were alive with Croatoan Indians, hunters and fishermen who scoured the maritime forests and the rich waters for bountiful fish and game. When the fair-skinned people with the blue eyes arrived from the giant crafts on the waves, my Indian ancestors were intrigued, and being polite, welcomed the visitors to their island. They feasted together, they showed the guests their lovely island… and eventually, some of them fell in love."

When the colonists feared White had abandoned them, they returned to the friendly Croatoan Indians, Berry said, in what is now Buxton, NC.

Reports of blue-eyed Indians along the North Carolina coast go back as far as the Huguenots. European colonists from the 1600s until the middle 1700s would report encounters with blue or grey-eyed Indians who spoke Elizabethan English.

In 1699, Morgan Jones, a Welsh cleric, reported he was taken captive by the Tuscarora and feared for his life, but an Indian spoke to him in Welsh, assuring him that he would not be killed. And in 1701, British surveyor John

Lawson wrote of members of the Hatteras tribe living on Roanoke Island who had grey eyes and claimed their ancestors were white people.

Despite the historical and Native Americans claims that Indians took the colonists in, many declared the Lost Colony one of history's greatest mysteries. Until last year.

In November 2020, Scott Dawson, president and founder of the Croatoan Archaeological Society, Inc., along with archaeologist William Kelso, found evidence of 16th century English material – such as pottery shards and a rapier hilt – in two separate areas within 50 miles of the English settlement. This, the men say, is proof the English settlers moved in with and were assimilated by nearby Native American tribes.

"Not only did we find sixteenth-century English artifacts in the Croatoan Indian villages but also evidence of assimilation. We now know not just where they went but also what happened after they got there," Dawson said.

Kelso, in an interview with National Geographic said the recent discoveries "solve one of the greatest mysteries in early American history--the odyssey of the Lost Colony."

But still there are those that don't buy it.

Dr. Charles Ewan, Director of the Phelps Archaeology Laboratory and Professor of

Anthropology at East Carolina University, said in an email interview that the mere presence of those artifacts doesn't prove that's where the colonists settled.

"The ceramics found at Site X and later Site Y in Bertie County are very early. However, those ceramics are found in the 16th AND 17th century, so they are not necessarily from the Lost Colonists. Jamestown and other colonists in the North Carolina/Virginia area could have traded them to the natives," he said.

There are many theories on what happened, he said, but no real proof of anything.

"They went to Croatan (Hatteras Island) and merged with the Indians, they went inland and merged with the Natives, they went north to the Chesapeake and were killed by the Indians, they tried to sail back to England and didn't make it, the Spanish found them and killed them, and other variants on those themes," he said. "Any or none of those ideas might be correct. We simply don't know. When you have a very limited amount of actual data you can take it in many directions and people have. We need to find the original settlement (100 years of looking at Fort Raleigh has not turned it up) and then figure out what happened next."

And the mere existence of grey-eyed or blue-eyed Indians isn't proof that the Lost Colony settlers lived out their days assimilated with the Croatoan tribe, he said.

"The idea that the grey-eyed Indians (Lawson's actual quote) were descendants of the Lost Colony is not well supported," he said. "First, Lawson only heard about them, he never actually saw them. Second, if true, it doesn't necessarily mean they are Lost Colonists offspring. There were many opportunities to interact with Europeans before Lawson is in the area at the turn of the 18th century."

The Dark Watchers

Dark Watchers – From Santa Lucia Mountains of California onto the Pages of Classic American Writers

For more than 300 years, people have looked up into the rural mountains of California to see tall, dark figures staring back at them only to watch them disappear moments later.

The Dark Watchers, as they're called, appear between late afternoon and twilight to visitors to the rural Santa Lucia Mountains. Witnesses from Native Americans to American writers have reported seeing the figures lingering on the mountaintops, seemingly silently watching those below.

The Santa Lucia Mountains stretch along the California coast from Monterey County up through central San Luis Obispo County. In the early days of the state, they presented a challenge to the Spanish explorers making their way to the ocean.

As these explorers made their way up the mountains in the 1700s, they reported seeing the dark figures, and named them "Los Vigilantes Oscuros" – literally "the dark watchers". Later, as American settlers made their way over the mountains, they too reported the feeling of being watched from above.

"What have come to be known as the "Dark Watchers" are typically said to be very tall humanoid entities ranging in height from 7 feet tall all the way up to around 15 feet tall, dressed all in black and wearing flowing cloaks and wide brimmed hats, with many sightings also mentioning some sort of staves or sticks in the beings' hands," Brent Swancer, wrote on Mysterious Universe.com.

"Facial features are not typically seen, and they are almost always silent, enigmatic figures usually seen at a distance up on ridges silhouetted against the darkening twilight sky, always at around dusk or dawn, quietly looking over and surveying their domain with unknowable purpose and often vanishing in the blink of an eye, especially if one is to try and draw closer," he wrote.

Legend says they are a group of migratory entities that stalk travelers along the mountain range, endowed with exceptional hearing, and impeccable eyesight. They prefer, paranormal researchers, like Michael Chen with Beyond Science, say, to reveal themselves only to travelers with carrying simple possessions, like hats and walking sticks, instead of high-tech equipment.

The figures have even made their way into literature. Author John Steinbeck mentions the watchers in **his short story "Flight."**

> *"Pepé looked suspiciously back every minute or so, and his eyes sought the tops of the ridges ahead,"* Steinbeck wrote. *"Once, on a white barren spur, he saw a black figure for a moment; but he looked quickly away, for it was one of the dark watchers. No one knew who the watchers were, nor where they lived, but it was better to ignore them and never to show interest in them. They did not bother one who stayed on the trail and minded his own business."*

Steinbeck's mother, Olive Hamilton, was a believer in the Dark Watchers. Thomas Steinbeck, John Steinbeck's son, said that his grandmother often told tales of her days as a young teacher, riding through the remote woods of the mountains on her way to teach. She told him that she saw the watchers several times and even traded with them, leaving gifts of fruit, nuts and flowers in a shaded alcove near Mule Deer Canyon, and receiving gifts from the watchers on her return trip.

And California poet Robison Jeffers mentions them in his poem, "Such Counsels You Gave to Me," where he wrote, "...he thought it might be one of the watchers, who are often seen in this length of coast-range, forms that look human to human eyes, but certainly are not human. They come from behind ridges to watch."

What they really are, said Brian Dunning, publisher of *Skeptoid Magazine*, is unknown.

"Most likely, many different things are likely behind

what various eyewitnesses have interpreted as Dark Watcher sightings," Dunning said in an email interview. "Probably some have been caused by shadows, tricks of the light, or trees. Probably some have been sightings of actual people or animals who were standing up there for a moment. Probably some have been people who thought they saw something out of the corner of their eye which disappeared when they turned to look. Probably some have been something I haven't thought of. There's no way to know."

Popular theories suggest the Dark Watchers are merely the result of pareidolia – the psychological phenomenon where the human brain seeks out recognizable and familiar patterns and shapes in unclear or unfamiliar images. Others say they are nothing more than hallucinations brought on by the lack of oxygen in higher elevations, and exhaustion.

Still others suggest that the phenomenon is an optical illusion where the observer's magnified shadow is seen on the clouds, which amplifies the shadow's size before it evaporates. Known as the **"Brocken Specter"**, the phenomenon was identified in the Brocken peak of the Harz Mountains in Germany.

"When the Sun is low and the conditions are right, a shadow is cast by the walker onto the mist, making it appear as if a tall, shadowy figure is watching them from nearby," said James Felton, a senior editor on the website IFLScience.com. "The water droplets that make up the mist can shift around, causing a disorientating effect, as though the shadow is moving, sometimes towards the observer. So, people are literally being scared by their own shadows."

Others believe the phenomenon can be caused by infrasound. Infrasound is sound between 7 and 19 Hz, just below the range of normal human hearing, and can be generated by wind, among other things.

In 2003, a psychologist and paranormal debunker Richard Wiseman and several of his British colleagues conducted an infrasound experiment. In it they subjected some 700 people to a concert featuring four pieces of music – two of which contained 17 Hz tones at a volume just at the edge of human hearing. As a result, some 22% of the audience reported feeling anxious, uneasy, or fearful. Others reported a pressure on their chest or chills running up and down their spine.

Wiseman told the British Association for the Advancement of Science, "These results suggest that low frequency sound can cause people to have unusual experiences even though they cannot consciously detect infrasound."

A later British study in 2008 by psychologist Christopher French found that when he put volunteers in a "haunted" room rigged with infrasonic generators, "Most people reported at least some slightly odd sensation, such as a presence or feeling dizzy, and some reported terror, which we hadn't expected."

For now, however, no one knows for sure whether infrasound, optical illusions or a lack of oxygen are to blame. In fact, no one knows for sure what the Dark Watchers are, where they come from or where they go when they disappear. While it is likely the phenomenon is scientifically explained away as the brain playing tricks on people, if they are real, they have been wise enough to leave no tangible evidence of their existence – save, perhaps, for a few offerings of fruit to an author's mother.

INDEX

A

Aliens, 52, 54, 71, 72, 139
Appalachia, 138
Arkansas, 10, 12

B

Bell Witch, 128, 130, 131
Bell, John, 128, 129, 130
Big Muddy, 84, 85, 86, 87, 88
Bigfoot, 10, 17, 20, 21, 22, 25, 26, 27, 28, 29, 30, 31, 84, 85, 96, 98, 122, 127
Blenko, 96, 97
Blue-eyed Indians, 155, 157, 159
Boggy Creek, Legend of, 9, 10, 11, 17
Bunny Man, 150, 151, 152, 153

C

Cattle Mutilations, 17, 48, 49, 50, 51, 54, 55
Cherokee, 120, 121, 137
Chicago, 42, 57, 58, 59, 62, 63
Christian, R. C., 119
Connecticut, 131
Croatoan, 156, 157, 158, 159
Crybaby Bridge, 134

D

Dakota Indians, 43, 44
Derenberger, Woodrow, 106
Diana of the Dunes, 17, 57, 58, 60, 65
DNA, 20, 23, 24, 25, 31, 46, 141
Dunning, Brian, 54, 113

E

Edgar, Zelia, 109

F

FBI, 52, 55, 148
Flatwoods Monster, 17, 82, 90, 95, 96, 97, 98
Fouke Monster, 10, 11, 12

G

Georgia Guidestones, 17, 116, 117, 118, 139
Gray, Alice, 57, 58, 64

H

Hannah Cranna, 131, 133
Hellier, 113, 144, 145
Howe, Linda Moulton, 49
Hynek, J. Allen, 93

I

Illinois, 28, 84
Indiana, 17, 57, 59, 62, 64, 65
Indrid Cold, 108, 109, 110, 111, 112, 113
Iowa, 100, 103

K

Keel, John, 39, 111

159

Kentucky, 9, 15, 17, 20, 21, 22, 23, 25, 26, 27, 30, 31, 68, 71, 121, 139, 140, 142, 145

L

La Mala Hora, 134, 135, 136
Lake Pepin, 17, 43, 44, 45, 47
Lanulos, 110, 112, 113
Little Green Men, 17, 68, 127
Lost Colony, 155, 156, 158, 159, 160

M

Marcum, Thomas, 25
Maryland, 75, 77, 78, 79, 80, 82, 150
Meth Hogs, 139, 141, 142
Minnesota, 16, 43, 44, 46, 52
Mothman, 16, 17, 33, 36, 37, 38, 39, 40, 41, 42, 82, 97, 98, 104, 111, 127

N

New Jersey, 76, 78, 111, 146
Newkirk, Greg, 144
Newkirk, Greg and Dana, 113

O

Oregon, 28, 48, 50, 51

P

Pepie, 17, 43, 44, 45, 46
Pierce, Charles B., 11
Project Blue Book, 93, 94

R

Roosevelt, Teddy, 78

S

Silver Bridge, 38, 39, 40
Skeptoid Magazine, 113
Smiling Man, 106
Smithsonian, 78
Snallygaster, 75, 76, 77, 78, 79, 80, 81, 82, 83
Spearfinger, 136, 137, 138
Sutton, Lucky, 69
Swamp Stalker, 10

T

Taylor, Kandiss, 118
Tennessee, 38, 128, 130, 131, 137
Texarkana, 11, 12, 13
Thomason, Harry, 12

V

Van Meter Visitor, 100, 102, 103

W

Washington, D.C., 72, 150
Watcher, the, 139, 147, 149
West Virginia, 33, 34, 36, 37, 38, 39, 78, 79, 80, 82, 90, 91, 96, 97, 98, 106, 111
Wilson, Paul, 63
Witches, 128

Made in the USA
Middletown, DE
13 August 2024

58735690R00091